D0176212

Toddler

Real-life Stories of Those Fickle,
Irrational, Urgent, Tiny People We Love

Toddler

Real-life Stories of Those Fickle,
Irrational, Urgent, Tiny People We Love

EDITED BY JENNIFER MARGULIS, PH.D.

SEAL PRESS

TODDLER: REAL-LIFE STORIES OF THOSE FICKLE, IRRATIONAL, URGENT,
TINY PEOPLE WE LOVE

Copyright © 2003 by Jennifer Margulis

Published by Seal Press
An Imprint of Avalon Publishing Group Incorporated
1400 65th Street, Suite 250
Emeryville, CA 94608
www.sealpress.com

"Willy Walks" by Joyce Maynard originally appeared in *Domestic Affairs: Enduring
the Pleasures of Motherhood and Family Life.* Copyright © 1987 by Joyce Maynard.
Reprinted by permission of the author.

"Walking" by Louise Erdrich originally appeared in *The Blue Jay's Dance.* Copyright
© 1995 by Louise Erdrich. Reprinted by permission of HarperCollins.

"In Child Time" by Alexandra Kennedy originally appeared in *FamilyFun* Magazine. Copyright © 2000 by *FamilyFun.*

Library of Congress Cataloging-in-Publication Data

Toddler : life stories of those fickle, irrational, urgent, tiny people we love/edited by
    Jennifer Margulis
        p.cm.
    ISBN 1-58005-093-X (pbk.)
        1. Toddlers--Anecdotes. 2.Parent and child--Anecdotes. I. Margulis, Jennifer.

HQ774.5.T58 2003
649'.122--dc21

                                                                    2003057297

9 8 7 6 5 4 3 2

Designed by Paul Paddock
Printed in the United States of America by Berryville Graphics

For My Father

Contents

Introduction

Jennifer Margulis

FOR MONTHS AFTER HER BIRTHDAY, whenever anyone asked my daughter, "How are you?" she would reply, "I'm two," as if two were not an age but a state of being.

At the dinner table she insists that she does not like pizza. She grumps and fusses and spends twenty minutes scraping a chair that is twice as big as she is over the floor to another part of the dining room, "to get out from the way of Daddy."

"Are you mad at Daddy?" I ask. She opens her eyes wide and nods her head slowly, mouthing *"yes,"* realizing that the pause in her response makes for good drama and that she has our full attention.

"Why, honey?" asks my husband, concerned.

"Because," she points, "I want some of that pizza."

Like my daughter, every toddler has her own ontology. Most are adamant about their ways of seeing the world, although their views on food, clothes, sleep, and who drives the car may shift in seconds. They wreak havoc on the lives of even the most organized adults. They pull credit cards out of wallets, practice undressing themselves in public, and feel completely uninhibited about exhibiting their bodily excretions. Toddlers seem to do everything, even sleep, with urgency.

Parenting a whole person who is only two feet two inches tall but who has already developed an absolute yet constantly fluctuating worldview is often fascinating but not always easy. Indeed, caring for these impatient creatures is often so intense that we parents sometimes have trouble stepping back from the urgency of our children's toddlerhood to reflect on it.

But fickle, irrational, urgent, tiny people that they are, toddlers are also great muses. Poised between the baby's world and the child's world, toddlers teach us to take joy in the roundness and the texture of a small yellow rubber ball, in the comfort of an elbow pad posing as a yarmulke attached by a bobby pin, in the warm smell of a soft blanket. They may ignore us much of the time but they see things, beautiful things, in the world—"Mr. Golden Sun, Daddy!" my two-year-old exclaims, pointing to a tile mosaic that we just walked over without noticing. With the shortest attention spans in the world, toddlers pay attention to what you say to them, and then talk back to you in your own voice, with your own intonation, and in words you wish had not come from your mouth. They exasperate us, devastate us, defy us, yet they fill us with fresh wonder.

This book is a collection of stories about that devastation and wonder. It is not a how-to book: there are literally hundreds of books and magazines out there that advise parents about toddlers— how to stop Joey from playing with his privates in public, how to curtail Ryan's nighttime wanderings, and how to keep Annie from hoarding dried apricots in her mouth for hours. Instead, this is a book of real stories by real people about things that happen in their lives. Reflecting the changing demographics of parenting, many of these stories are written by fathers.

In "Mokeeho" we read about a young mother who loses her sight the same day her son is born and has to negotiate parenting her toddler blind; in "Pretender to the Throne" about a father whose curious two-year-old keeps him from being able to accomplish his task at hand in the bathroom; and in "Bedtime for Milo" about an exhausted mother whose toddler defies all the endings in picture-book tales and refuses to sleep through the night. As varied as the toddlers whose antics they describe, these stories give readers the chance to peek into the lives of other parents and share their joy, sorrow, frustration, and delight.

Since emerging into toddlerhood, my daughter herself has recognized the importance of stories. Every night before we put her in her crib we would tell her the story of herself by recounting to her all of the things she had done that day. It was her favorite part of our nighttime ritual and it was as hard for her to let go of the story as it was for her to let go of the day. "Day," she would whisper, wanting us to tell her about her adventures one more time, "more day."

Just shy of three, she now wants to hear stories about everything, including herself. She asks us to tell her about Daddy when his name was Jimmy, about Winnie-the-Pooh when his toes were cold, about her stuffed bear Jessica when she had a baby, and about the banjo when it went to the park with Jimmy, Winnie-the-Pooh, and Jessica Bear. Tired from telling stories while I am strolling her and her baby sister home, I plead for a pause. She waits less than thirty seconds and asks, "Is there a story in your mouth to tell me now?"

During more than five years of gestating and parenting, I have come to share my daughter's need for stories. I have found that the stories of other parents, and grandparents, and teachers, and strangers who smile sympathetically on the street have been much more helpful, reassuring, and interesting than the more impersonal advice often found in parenting books and magazine articles. Hungry for those kinds of stories, I conceived of this book the week after my second child, Athena, was born. Exhausted, sore-breasted, and sleep-deprived, I sat nursing my new baby one morning during a full-blown New England snowstorm. My husband bundled our older daughter, Hesperus, into five layers of clothing—he is originally from Buffalo and knows how to dress for snow—and dutifully trudged out into the storm to take her to music class and give me some time alone with Athena. Two minutes later they were back. Hesperus was screaming. James was crying.

Nineteen months old and relatively new to walking, Hesperus had slipped on the snow and hurt herself. She was not able to stand up. Her leg was fractured and for ten days she could not walk. All of a sudden we found ourselves with two babies in diapers who both needed to be carried, one who smelled of amniotic fluid and the other who weighed almost twenty-five pounds. "How do people do this?" my husband and I wondered. We called up everyone we knew who had small children. "How do people do this?" we asked. I gobbled up books like *Mothers Who Think* and *Between Mothers and Sons,* anthologies of true stories about the experience of motherhood. But I needed a book like those with stories about toddlers and could not find one. *Toddler* is the book I wished I had—a book for parents and other adults whose lives are enriched and riled by toddlers; a book for those who want to read about what others are experiencing and who might find a bit of themselves on these pages.

Like many of the contributors to this anthology, I did the writing and editing for this book on stolen time—snatches of time while my two girls were napping, short stretches of time after they went to bed but before the baby woke to nurse, tiny bits of time while my one-year-old wobbled around the house pulling books off shelves exclaiming "ut oh!" with every crash and my two-year-old sat on my lap at the computer "playing" with the keyboard, and the more luxurious time I had on Saturday mornings when I left incoherent instructions for my sleepy husband and ran to the public library. One of the many things my two toddling muses have taught me is to make the most of my time. Like many parents who find themselves strangely more efficient with less time and less sleep than they have ever had before, I use every free second like it is my last.

Like me, some of the contributors to this book were professional writers before they had children. Others have found themselves inspired by parenting to write for the first time in their lives. Together we try to capture these best and worst of times. In these stories we describe the triumphs and defeats that come along with this lifelong job, given only to amateurs, about which none of us really has any idea before we begin.

Walking

Louise Erdrich

To PULL HERSELF UPRIGHT, to strain upward, to climb, has been baby's obsession for the past three months and now, on her first birthday, it is that urge I celebrate and fear. She has pulled herself erect by the strings of her sister's hair, by using my clothes, hands, earrings, by the edges and the rungs and the unstable handles of the world. She has yanked herself up, stepped, and it is clear from her grand excitement that walking is one of the most important things we ever do. It is raw power to go forward, to lunge, catching at important arms and hands, to take control of the body, tell it what to do, to leave behind the immobility of babyhood. With each step she swells, her breath goes ragged and her eyes darken in a shine of happiness. A glaze of physical joy covers her, moves through her, more intense than the banged forehead, bumped chin, the bruises and knocks and losses, even than the breathtaking falls and solid thumps, joy more powerful than good sense.

It would seem she has everything she could want—she is fed, she is carried, she is rocked, put to sleep. But no, *walking* is the thing, the consuming urge to seize control. She has to walk to gain entrance to the world. From now on, she will get from here to there more and more by her own effort. As she goes, she will notice worn grass, shops or snow or the shapes of trees. She will walk for reasons other than to get somewhere in particular. She'll walk to think or not to think, to leave the body, which is often the same as becoming at one with it. She will walk to ward off anger in its many forms. For pleasure, purpose, or to grieve. She'll walk until the world slows down, until her brain lets go of everything behind and until her eyes see only the next step. She'll walk until her feet hurt, her muscles tremble, until her eyes are numb with looking. She'll walk until her sense of balance is the one thing left and the rest of the world is balanced, too, and eventually, if we do the growing up right, she will walk away from us.

Everything Is Full of Dada

Scott Samuelson

LIKE COUNTLESS FIRST-TIME FATHERS BEFORE ME, I was gleeful when the first articulate, controlled noise from my baby's mouth was "Dada." Irene looked up at me one day and quite knowingly, or so it seemed to me then, said, "Dada." She too must have been gleeful at the occasion, for, in fact, she said, "Dadadadadadadada," as if rejoicing in her discovery of my identity. I suppressed the desire to gloat to Helen. When I casually brought it up, she replied, "Yes, I know. Isn't that sweet? She loves her Daddy." With a touch of jealousy, she added, "I understand it's the easiest syllable for a baby to pronounce."

I was a little disheartened when later that day I found Irene in her highchair calling her sliced peaches "Dada." When I overheard her calling her Curious George toy "Dada," I consoled myself: she was pretending the monkey was me. That the cat was also named "Dada" was harder to account for; so was the fact that strangers, various chew-toys, and balls of lint she grubbed on the floor had all become "Dada." Even Mama was "Dada." "Dada" also seemed to signify invisible presences, for she would murmur my title even when there was nothing in her line of vision I could identify as a nameable object.

I admit the thought crossed my mind that she was not in fact denominating me with her reduplicated syllable but merely babbling as babies uncomprehendingly do.

One day while playing with her on the floor in front of our bookshelves, I considered the troublingly large area covered by her newfound term of endearment. Even before my daughter was born I had been curious about our strange ability to pass from the wilderness of wordlessness into a linguistic home. How do raw sounds attach to the world? How does shaped breath come to mean something to us? The hypothesis of Giambattista Vico, an eighteenth-century Neapolitan philosopher, had always fascinated me, although until Irene's Dada phase I had never seriously entertained it as true. Vico speculated that the first humans spontaneously invented language when they heard thunder. Overcome with fear and awe, they imitated the booming sound in speech: Pa-Pa. This word signified the phenomenon itself and the power behind the phenomenon, the Father God.

Vico, as I recalled, quoted a line from Virgil to illustrate his further point that the word "Pa-Pa" (it could just as easily have been "Da-Da") at first stood for all things. In this primitive language, the whole world was represented as being occupied by a single god and eventually by multiple gods. As Irene fidgeted with some plastic rings, I took the Roman poet's *Eclogues* off my shelf and looked up the quoted line: *"Jovis omnia plena"*—literally, everything is full of Jove. That explained it. Everything is full of Dada. My baby girl had magically retraced the most ancient of ancient history. She had invoked my name and applied its wondrous syllables to the whole wondrous world. I, Jove-like, looked happily down to share my discovery with her, wordlessly. Her lips began to move. A word—the word—was forming on them. With a look of awe and love on her face, she looked up at me and muttered, "Mama."

That was a few months ago. She now has several words. Her most reliable, I have to admit, has been "Mama." Whenever she is in distress, she reaches out her arms to Helen and calls out, "Mama!" She also says things like "cat," "hi," "bye-bye," "Oo-ee" (to denominate the music of Louis Armstrong, our cat named Louis, and sometimes other animals) and—of course—"Dada." (Helen and I have a debate about the extent to which Irene's other sounds can qualify as words. Is, for instance, her pronouncing "duh" in the vicinity of a duck sufficient grounds for concluding that she knows the word "duck"?) Besides "Mama," her other words are used correctly only sometimes. They all have been known to signify whatever happens to be in front of her. She is slowly learning the conditions of their proper usage. The world is being emptied of Jove. Any day now "Dada" will be just me.

Lessons from Snake Boy

Karen C. Driscoll

I HAVE TWO-YEAR-OLD TWINS AND A SIX-MONTH-OLD. I don't go anywhere by myself without a double stroller, a backpack, a diaper bag, and a Snugli. Throw a purse, a cell phone, a couple of distraction toys, several changes of clothes, and a pacifier on top of the pile and you have the reason I usually don't go anywhere at all. But today I'm feeling ambitious and we're going to the zoo. I double-check to make sure everyone has been changed, cleaned, fed, and juiced. Times three. I'm exhausted and we haven't even left the driveway.

Once we reach the zoo I put on the front-pack and put the baby into it, adjusting and readjusting the straps and buckles so I don't feel like my shoulders are going to snap. I open the trunk and the double stroller falls out of the car with a crash, narrowly missing me. By the time I have it set up and the girls are out of their car seats and buckled into the stroller and I've ascertained that I have my mountain of necessary stuff crammed into the stroller with them, my T-shirt is soaked with sweat. I straighten up slowly, stretching my back, and take a deep breath. We're finally here! But that deep breath, combined with my son's kicking me happily, *thud thud thud,* right in the bladder brings on an unwelcome realization.

Using a public bathroom while wielding a double stroller complete with four grabbing hands and two running commentaries probably does not rank very high on anyone's list of favorite pastimes. It ranks rock bottom on mine.

"Look!" Brittany hollers, leaning over the side of the stroller and snatching up an errant length of toilet paper from the ground. While I'm busy disentangling her I realize I have given Holly total access to that most amazing of all wonders, the sanitary napkin receptacle. She's flipped the lid up and down, up and down, before I even realize what she's touching.

"No!" I screech, "Dirty! Don't touch that!" Holly is undeterred.

"What's in here, Mommy?" she asks, poising her hand to answer the question for herself. I lunge across the stroller, successfully apprehending her overly curious arm, but forgetting that I have a twenty-pound infant strapped to my body. Robbie starts screaming at full volume as his head makes contact with the stall's metal wall. For a second I'm sure I've given him a concussion. But no, he's okay, just jostled. "Sorry, sorry," I croon to him while at the same time shooting my daughters a malevolent glare and hissing "Do. Not. Touch. Another. Thing. Understand?" in between apologies. I start to entertain the imminent possibility of my bladder exploding into a billion bits. All I can say is thank God for elastic waistbands and all the leg-squat exercises I once did to improve my skiing. Little did I know those exercises would prove most useful for helping to keep my bladder intact while avoiding any physical contact whatsoever with a dirty toilet, while holding an overly large baby, while doing damage control with twin toddlers (who are at this point asking me loud, detailed questions about exactly what I'm doing). And so, a good half-hour after we rolled into the rest room, we roll out again, my organs unexploded and my offspring's hands sanitized.

We enter the Reptile Room. When my eyes adjust to the murky light I see a scruffy-looking employee stacking boxes. He's young, scraggly-haired, and has more earrings than I do. The girls are already staring, mesmerized, at the undulating bodies of several surprisingly active boa constrictors. This is the first time they've ever seen a snake. I roll the stroller up close and they bang excitedly on the glass cage with their small fists. "Hi! Hi!" they shout. A sign at the top of the enclosure reads "Do Not Tap on Glass—What Would You Do If it Broke?" I back up the stroller.

At least four very large boas are gazing at my children with extreme interest. I'm suddenly morbidly fascinated.

"Can they bite? Or do they just squeeze?"

"Oh, they've got a whole mouthful of teeth. Make you bleed like a son of a gun." Snake Boy says it like a boa bite is one of the top coolest things that could happen to you. He holds up a scarred hand. At this moment my six-month-old makes a noise from the front-pack like his intestines are rupturing. I hear the soft plopping sounds at my feet that tell me the contents of his diaper have just bypassed containment. I sigh, survey my mountain of stuff, and glumly realize that "extra-outfit-for-baby" didn't make it onto the pile. At least I've got diaper wipes. I go to work. Snake Boy doesn't skip a beat. "You ever touch a snake before?" he asks me, hovering while I kneel over my son. I'm just realizing that the boxes he's haphazardly stacking contain one large snake each. His hand rests casually on one of the lids.

Suddenly my son is looking just a little too plumply pink and prey-like, lying at the bellies of several hundred pounds of serpent. He's not perfectly clean but I scoop him up anyway. I can feel the skin on my neck prickle. "Actually," I admit, "snakes scare me." Snake Boy looks sympathetic, nodding. "You know," he says in a confidential tone, "I spent my entire life being scared of snakes, and now look at me. It's crazy—I'm a snake handler, and I love it!"

I felt the same way about children, and then I had three babies in eighteen months. I was standing in line for a serene Mary Cassatt painting and ended up with something that looks more like Edvard Munch's "Scream."

"Hey girls! Wanna see a really big toad?" Four little eyes dutifully gaze at the grotesque amphibian he's holding. Watery drops fall from its body. "See that, that's poison," he says almost reverently, and then tosses the animal into a cage. He's just touched the toad with his bare hands, and the poison has dripped onto the carpet a few feet from where my son's head rested as I changed his diaper.

"My hand's gonna start burning like crazy if I don't go and wash it off. But all things considered, it's a pretty small price to pay." He actually winks at me. "You probably know what I mean," he says and nods toward my children. I look at him closely. There's none of the "poor you" I frequently get from strangers. There's only recognition. He holds out his hand and gestures toward the messy diaper. "I'll take that for you," he says and I hand it to him without apologizing for its untouchable condition. I replay my day so far: the exasperation of gathering and traveling with so much paraphernalia; the difficulty, with three kids in tow, of doing something as simple as using the bathroom; and the joys of Reptile Room diaper disasters.

There is no such thing as an easy outing with these three, and I frequently feel like throwing my hands up and waving the white diaper of surrender, even when we stay home. I find myself yearning for a day I simultaneously dread, when my children are older and don't rely on me so heavily. No stroller to push. No baby to carry. A day when the weight of three small bodies hanging from my body—my neck, legs, and arms locked in the vice-like grip of pudgy toddler-hands—is gone. The freedom of moving from being the center of three universes to a star on the periphery of a triple galaxy, of three children going from needing me too much to needing me too little. I can't help but wonder, as I think about how many times today I will pry tiny fingers from squeezing too hard around my neck so that I can breathe, if the weight of that freedom will feel more like emptiness. If that emptiness will feel like suffocation. But I'm still looking at the cheerful Snake Boy with the poison on his fingers and the soiled diaper in his hand, and he's still smiling at me. "It's a pretty small price to pay," he's said. The truth of his words transcends the cliché.

The girls are laughing, pointing here and there, eyes wide. My son is kicking his legs and making exuberantly appreciative gurgling noises from the front-pack. They are so excited about the newness of every experience, so thrilled by life itself, they can barely contain themselves. For a very short time, I get to be a part of it all.

Lessons from Snake Boy

"I definitely know what you mean," I say to Snake Boy. And I do.

"I thought you probably did," he says over his shoulder as he slam-dunks the dirty diaper into a garbage can and heads for the sink.

Small voices around my knees clamor for more animals. We head out into the brilliant sunshine.

A Tale of Two Preschools

Hope Edelman

IT WAS THE KIND OF PRESCHOOL I would have created myself, if I'd aspired to create a preschool. The colors were bright but not too bright; the classrooms vibrant but not overwhelming. The backyard featured a blue playhouse and a soft carpet of bark chips. Unlike so many buildings in Los Angeles, this one looked as if people actually used it. It was a low-slung, unobtrusive Frank Lloyd Wright design that seemed compatible with the structured Montessori plan. The Sri Lankan codirector greeted me warmly at the front door and walked me through the three rooms, where children of more races and ethnicities than I could easily identify worked side by side. It looked like a tiny, welcoming UN. The whole package made me so happy I almost started to cry.

We didn't get in.

To be accurate, our twenty-month-old daughter, Maya, didn't get in. She was wait-listed. For the following year.

Here on the west side of Los Angeles, being wait-listed for preschool is something like a cross between purgatory and grammar-school gym class. You spend a lot of anxious time standing around, wondering what you did wrong. Did I have a grape juice stain on my blouse during the interview? Did I write the wrong bank account number on the application? A better question might be, Why, exactly, does a preschool need my bank account number? But never mind. You don't ask questions when you're filling out the forms. Competition for slots in the city's most desirable preschools is fierce. You want your family to stand out, but not for the wrong reasons.

Just getting to this point had been odyssey enough. For the past year, my husband and I had been hotly debating whether to send Maya, our only child, to preschool at age two. He was raised in Israel, where most children go to a *gan,* a neighborhood daycare center, starting at seven months. The idea of keeping a child home was unnatural and nonsensical to him. But I was raised in suburban New York in the 1960s, where few mothers worked and children did a year of preschool at age four, if at all. Also, I worked from a home office and had a reliable nanny. Our late-night conversations, full of agenda, started going something like this:

"She's bored at home."

"She can't be bored. She's not even *two.*"

"I think she needs more stimulation."

"What stimulation? She's *not even two.*"

"Well, she wants to be with other kids."

On this count, I had to concede. Every time we drove by a park, Maya lifted her arms plaintively toward the swings and cried, "Kidz! Kidz!" She would toddle up to small groups of children, bursting with self-confidence, and quickly integrate into their play. I knew these were signs of preschool readiness and so, eventually, I gave in.

By this time, however, I was way behind the curve. By the time my husband and I agreed to send Maya to school two mornings a week she was a whopping nineteen months old, practically a senior citizen by admissions standards. At one school I learned I should have joined the toddler group six months earlier to be considered for a slot; at others, parents had started mailing in applications soon after their children were born. I couldn't compete with that kind of foresight, even if I'd wanted to.

When we discovered we no longer had even the illusion of choice, our standards changed dramatically. Student-teacher ratio? Music programs? Ha. Suddenly, the only criteria that mattered was an empty spot.

Fortunately, we live in a canyon town with a free-spirited sensibility, a place where rules are often flexible and, at best, nominally enforced. There are four local preschools, though I'd already dismissed three of them as either too expensive, too flaky, or too funky. The fourth I'd scratched from my list when I heard it followed the RIE (Resources for Infant Educarers) program. RIE stresses giving children uninterrupted playtime and freedom to explore, and treating them with trust and respect. It sounded good, in theory. But my friends who'd done RIE Mommy & Me had entered the groups as normal English-speaking mothers and emerged twelve weeks later addressing their children in painfully slow, clearly articulated sentences packed with adjectives. *Can you put. The square, red block. On the big, blue. Blanket?* It was actually a little creepy. Panic, however, is the mother of re-evaluation. I called the RIE preschool in early August and asked if they still had space for the fall.

The director called back three weeks later. She taught the two-year-olds and couldn't take any more children, she explained, because one of her entering students had been injured that summer and might need extra attention. But by early winter she might be ready to add another child.

"You'll start a child in the middle of the year?" I asked.

"Sure," she said.

Her voice was mellifluous and calming. She didn't seem addicted to adjectives. I'd seen her around town a few times, a middle-aged woman with long, wavy hair and flowing print skirts. She looked cheerful and pleasant, like the kind of person who frequently said, "No problem," and meant it. While this should have been reassuring to me, it actually made me a little nervous. Flexibility has never been my strong point. "Laid-back" is not a term that has ever been used to describe me. Yet so much of the preschool admissions process depends more on the parent's presentation than on the child's. Whereas I'd previously worried about whether I looked professional or affluent enough for a West side preschool director, as I drove up to the RIE school I was strangely preoccupied with whether I appeared free-spirited and earthy enough to be accepted there.

The preschool was tucked away in a residential neighborhood, in a converted wooden house with a large sandbox and several small playhouses in the front yard. In the front room, a few children played on the carpet with vintage Fisher-Price toys that looked like they'd fetch a small fortune on eBay. Others were building a tower out of blocks. I waved at the director, who held a sobbing blond child on her shoulder. She smiled, and waved back.

One of my friends, an older mother, once told me it doesn't matter what kind of philosophy a preschool follows, or how new or orderly the facilities are. What really matters, she said, is the teacher. Find a warm, nurturing teacher who genuinely cares about students and your child will thrive. I thought about this as I observed how the RIE school director helped two children arguing over the same toy resolve the conflict themselves. I noticed that she toted the distressed child on her hip throughout my tour until he felt calm enough to join the other kids.

She asked me about Maya—How well could she express her needs? (Pretty well; she was highly verbal.) Did she have much play experience with children her age? (Just our Mommy & Me group and Gymboree.) She didn't ask to meet my husband. She didn't seem to care about what I did for a living, or what kind of education I'd received. It was, frankly, a relief to feel that the emphasis was being placed on the child, where it belonged.

On Maya's first morning at the RIE school I sat on a couch inside the classroom, on call to help her adjust. Instead, I acted as a one-person greeting committee for each small child she brought over with the introduction, "See this? This is my mom!" On the second morning, I offered to help pour juice at snack time and carry wet art projects outside to dry, while Maya pretended I wasn't there. By the third morning, she was totally absorbed with the other kids, her dark, curly hair indistinguishable in the little mob on the carpet. The director approached me on the couch. "It's time to go now," she said, gracious yet firm.

It was not the kind of preschool environment I'd once envisioned. There were no rows of orderly cubbies, or alphabet charts on the wall. The kids had names like Ocean and Sky, and several of the mothers—none of them native Indians—wore *bindis* between their eyes. But as the months passed our kitchen walls filled up with drawings, I cooked potato latkes for the school's potluck luncheon, and we brought the class guinea pigs home for a night. When I dropped Maya off in the mornings I started staying a few extra minutes to push her on the swings, where I became friendly with an Italian mom who'd just traveled around the world with her husband and two-year-old son. I grew to love the place. When re-enrollment time arrived, I signed Maya up for the fall.

Then, in July, the Montessori school called.

They had a spot available for Maya in September, and they were looking forward to having her in class.

For several weeks, we waffled. We gave deposits to both schools, knowing we would lose money one way or the other, knowing it was a crappy thing to do to the school we didn't choose. Because we really couldn't choose. I couldn't bear the thought of leaving the RIE school. But Montessori embodied everything that had ever said "preschool" to me. The friendly codirector who seemed so enamored with the kids. The colorful alphabet posters on the wall. Those damn cubbies, which represented everything I liked so much about practicing responsibility and tidiness at school.

For a brief time in my twenties, I was in love with two men at the same time. One was a bond analyst on Wall Street who wore white shirts and dark suits, the other an aspiring writer who was partial to black Converse high-tops. Preschools, I came to realize, are a little bit like lovers. It's possible to give your heart to two at the same time.

In the end, it was Maya who helped us decide. One evening after dinner she walked up to me with a book and asked me to teach her to read. So we went for the Montessori school and its prereading curriculum. On the first day that fall, Maya's chin wobbled slightly when she bid me good-bye. Then she ran off into the play yard with the other kids.

I grew to love this school, too. The teachers were extraordinary, and the parents all accomplished and involved. I loved that this Montessori encouraged artwork and imaginative play, that Maya learned songs in Spanish and Sri Lankan, and that in her second year I had to sign her up for aftercare hours, not because I needed the childcare but because at the end of the school day she didn't want to leave.

We never had reason to doubt the decision we made. We see now, with the perfect vision of hindsight, that Maya was in the right place for her at age two, and moved to the right place for her at age three. Yet sometimes I still find myself driving out of my way so I can pass the RIE school. I slow down and open my window just to hear the sounds of children playing in the front yard. That's what I mean about preschools being like lovers. No matter how much you love the one you're with, a part of you never stops missing the one that got away.

The Dinner Hour

Jamie Pearson

"It's five o'clock," insists my daughter Avery with her usual authority. The strength of will and conviction of a three-year-old can be awe-inspiring, particularly by five o'clock. It's actually only 4·51 P.M., but after a day short on naps and long on spectacular potty training accidents, I feel entitled to round up. With my husband traveling for business, there will be no reinforcements. To Avery, five o'clock means one rapturous hour of television. Despite my previous ideals, I have made peace with television. I have also made peace with Happy Meals, vast quantities of Goldfish crackers, and talking Teletubby toys. Parenting is nothing if not humbling.

The program begins and Avery suddenly shrieks as if in physical pain. She wants a different show. A morning show. In the most soothing voice available to me at five o'clock, I explain my limited influence over both PBS programming and the planetary phenomenon of night following day. Avery bears my irony with stoicism, and I experience a moment of vertigo as she considers her next move. Cooperation or resistance? She wavers, and then relaxes into the couch. I'm flooded with relief. It's equally flattering and exhausting to be regarded as omnipotent. Next I wrestle my clingy eight-month-old son, Max, into a backpack carrier and slip it on. This particular piece of gear is intended for hiking. I'm planning to unload the dishwasher and make dinner. Feeling pleased with my ingenuity and with twenty-one pounds of teething baby on my back, I hike over to the dishwasher. As I bend down, Max shifts his weight for a better view. Perhaps he's never actually seen clean dishes before. I stumble, and narrowly avoid impaling myself on the top rack as the phone begins to ring. Max's pacifier falls out of his mouth and deep into the dishwasher.

Hopeful of any adult conversation, I hurry to the phone. It's the trainer I called in desperation when our previously housebroken dog began peeing on our bed, on my side. The trainer specializes in dog/baby adjustments. I explain the situation, and we agree that the dog has not made a successful dog/baby adjustment. Over Max's stream of discontented babble, the trainer ventures that our dog is distressed because he is never allowed in the house. I respectfully disagree, pointing out that he is never allowed in the house because he pees on our bed. The trainer is diplomatic, but I can't help feeling he's on the dog's side. He suggests that I tie the dog to myself by stringing his leash through my belt loop. If the dog doesn't feel excluded, he reasons, he won't feel stressed. If he doesn't feel stressed, he won't pee on the bed. As I recover the pacifier with a long-handled spatula, it occurs to me that the dog trainer probably doesn't have children. Mercifully, Max's chubby hand reaches over my shoulder and disconnects the phone before the trainer can offer further advice.

The Dinner Hour

With the dog now tied to my pants, I attempt to remove dinner from the oven. Max seems to be interested in touching all the hot things he can reach, so I clamp his hand between my teeth as I execute this complicated maneuver. Meanwhile, the smell of roast chicken tantalizes the already unstable dog. He races around my feet several times, cartoonishly tying me up with the leash. I am undeterred. Under extremely trying circumstances, practically combat conditions, I will be serving a real dinner. Chicken, potatoes, and green beans. I fantasize about telling my absent husband the details. How nutritious it was. How easy it was. For whatever reason, I am not dissuaded by the fact that Avery has never actually eaten any of these foods.

As Avery's program ends, I rush to untangle the dog's leash and settle Max in the highchair. Avery stalks into the kitchen like a force of nature, and conducts a suspicious inspection of the table. She demands pancakes. When I gently refuse, she collapses prostrate at my feet. I take a deep breath, silently willing myself to savor our idyllic family dinner. Max throws his sippy cup. Inevitably, it lands directly on Avery's head, and chaos ensues. In the split second it takes for me to retrieve the cup and comfort my hysterical daughter, the dog makes his move. He leaps onto my vacant chair and launches himself at the table, ransacking my plate before I can stop him. Stepping over my howling child to throw the dog outside, I think unkind thoughts about my husband and the dog trainer.

Avery sobs for a Band-Aid. This is problematic, as the cup has landed on the part of her head covered with hair. I try to get away with a pretend Band-Aid and a kiss, but this only enrages her more.

I run to the bathroom for real Band-Aids. Max starts screaming the moment I am out of sight. I return quickly, but he refuses to stay in the highchair, where he is vulnerable to being left alone, however briefly. I allow Avery to play with the entire box of Band-Aids. This renders the Band-Aids useless in terms of actual first aid, but seems to mollify her. I ignore this blatant metaphor of my parenting style. At a minimum, Avery seems to have forgotten her head injury as she decorates the kitchen table with Band-Aids.

The dog scratches maniacally on the back door, casting baleful looks at my defiled plate of chicken. I consider the dog-training implications of just letting him eat the rest of it. Avery looks up from her art project and announces that she is hungry. I bring her plastic Elmo plate with me to the stove, and pop a few cubes of cold chicken in my mouth. With Max firmly on my hip, I reach for the Bisquick and begin making pancakes one-handed.

Fly-fishing for Footwear

Peter W. Fong

THE LAST TIME WE DROVE THROUGH YELLOWSTONE, I got caught behind a motor yacht trolling for scenery at a leisurely fifteen knots. Instead of trying to pass, I laid off the accelerator and rolled down the windows. The hillsides below the summit of Mount Washburn were already tinged with the red of autumn. At eight thousand feet, the air smelled of fall, crisp and cool and faintly dusty, without the scent of growing things. To the east: the hulks of Druid Peak and the Thunderer glowering in the smoke of a late-season fire. To the south: forests of pine and fir like a ragged pelt on the flanks of the mountain, meadow grass gone golden with August, the Yellowstone River meandering through the Hayden Valley, and, creeping alongside the river, the glint of aluminum travel trailers in the setting sun.

Their sheepish procession reminded me of a day of fishing with my son, Dave, still in diapers then, on a stretch of the Madison that runs alongside the highway to West Yellowstone. It was a warm, breezy afternoon and I was wading wet, flipping a big caddis nymph into the deep runs, while Dave watched over my shoulder from the safety of the baby pack. As we worked our way downstream, a cow elk walked out into the water below us, her neck and ears twitching with flies. She dipped her muzzle into the water, tossed her head at the shimmery surface, scratched at her neck with one sharp hoof.

In minutes, the road was lined shoulder to shoulder with license plates from Illinois and Washington and California. Camera shutters shirred like locusts. The cow took a couple of prancing steps toward the far bank and shook with annoyance. Dave and I turned our backs to the crowd and kept fishing. I heard a splash nearby and to the right, like the swirl of a trout, and pivoted on the mossy rocks. "Did you hear that?" I asked him. "Was that a fish?"

"No," he said, then fell silent. I cast, letting the fly drift under a bathtub-sized patch of river weed and into a dark hole of water.

I was picking up the fly to cast again when Dave whimpered: "My sandal."

I repeated the word dumbly—sandal, sandal—before remembering the nearby splash. I reached behind me and tickled his right foot. It was bare. When I looked downstream, his sandal was bobbing twenty yards away and gaining speed, on a collision course with the fully grown and fully aggravated cow elk. I tried a couple of quick shuffling steps in that direction, then sent the fly out after it. But the beloved sandal was a small, rapidly dwindling target that changed course with each little finger of current. I threw a couple of big mends into the line and still missed by a foot. Dave's whimpering was more insistent now—"Get sandal, get sandal."

I took another look at the elk and decided she wouldn't much appreciate two humans churning downstream into her bath. So I made for shore and the camera-wielding tourists, charged up the bank, then shouldered my way onto the path that parallels the river. The wind was blowing up and across the current, slowing the sandal's progress enough for us to pull ahead, but also angling it into the deeper water midstream. Fifty yards behind the elk, I picked a gravelly spot and splashed in. The river was belt-high. Frightened trout fled for cover as we thrashed through ribbons of weed. My feet had just reached the lip of a dark trough when the sandal floated into arm's reach. I leaned over and gathered it in like a catcher pulling an outside pitch back toward the strike zone. Dave thrust his hands into the air and cheered loudly enough to turn a few cameras from the elk. I cheered too. The nearest onlookers gave us those benign and disconnected smiles that most folks reserve for fools and crazy people. But what did we care? We were flush with success, proud conspirators in a small but significant victory.

Caretaking

Dennis Donoghue

THE IN-GROUND POOL WAITS OVER MY PROPERTY LINE, just beyond the gap between the cedar tree and the honeysuckle bush. Fourteen-month-old Justina, drawn by the glint of sun off the pool ladder, streaks for the gap and reaches the concrete deck before I catch up to her.

My neighbor won't enclose his pool so I'm unrolling two hundred feet of coated wire fencing along the property line and staking it with metal poles every twelve feet or so. My other two daughters, Beatrice, three, and Apphia, two, never thought much of the pool. Apphia prefers to bolt down the driveway toward the street. She's the only one of the three I've lost for any length of time, a mind-numbing few minutes after I'd finished a road race when I took my eye off her to dig into a tub of ice for a fruit drink. She was wearing a YMCA T-shirt, like most of the kids there that Saturday morning, when she wandered away. Fighting panic, I darted back and forth, dragging Beatrice, who chewed on a bagel. I shouted Apphia's name as I wildly scanned the crowd for a kid with ringlet curls escaping the ponytail on top of her head. A helplessness filled me like nothing I'd ever felt before. There was a cop on detail, but I ran past him. I couldn't imagine telling my wife, Carla, who waited fifty yards away with Justina. Finally I found Apphia, alone by a rusty backstop, her fingers curled around the chain link. She was staring at something—a sparrow, a candy wrapper, the guy across the street mowing his lawn. Without speaking, I clutched her pudgy forearm and led her away, overwhelmed with relief.

At forty-six I wonder whether I am too old to be raising toddlers. My back aches every morning. Descending the stairs, I lean on the banister. In the kitchen I move slowly, stretch, drink black coffee. Up two hours before the kids for some time alone, I tell myself that I could not have done this as a younger man. I have patience now, insight. I think before I act. Then I remember the trip home from my mother-in-law's last week.

We were somewhere between Providence and Boston. Two hours into the ride and an hour to go, Apphia started screaming. Pure bursts of sound pierced my eardrums and fanned out inside my head. She did this, for fun, every few seconds, mile after mile. Asking her to stop challenged her to scream louder. With frayed nerves, I weaved our small van through thickening traffic. Finally, unable to bear another scream, I slammed the wheel and shouted, "Jesus Christ, shut the fuck up!"

Carla shot me a look.

"Clamp your hand over her mouth," I ordered my wife. "That'll keep her quiet."

"And keep it there for the next forty-five miles?" she asked.

In no time a toddler's behavior changes me into someone who can't control himself, who disgusts his wife and scares his children.

What am I doing, I ask myself, when similar screams while we're raking leaves entice me to join in? She screams, I scream, Beatrice and Justina join us; we toss leaves around, go night-night in the pile, jump up, and start screaming again.

That's the way it goes between us. I'm never quite sure how to act, never convinced that what I'm doing is what I ought to be doing. Half the time I'm screwing them up. The other half, I'm trying to keep them safe. It's not as if I've had lessons, and maybe I'm too old to learn.

Carla insists, for instance, that I stop peeing in front of them. She says the toddler book contends I might stimulate my children sexually in some unconscious way. "Quit it," she says, "or else close the door." But they'll be in the tub, splashing away, when the daily quart of green tea I drink for prostate health forces me to do something. I can't hold it and I can't leave to use the downstairs bathroom. So while Beatrice hunts for the translucent pink soap beneath the sudsy surface, Apphia scrubs the tiles with a washcloth, and Justina in her bath seat sucks on a rubber penguin, I push myself off the bath mat, lift the seat, and go. Of course they stop what they're doing, turn, and study me.

Awkward and self-conscious, possibly inflicting psychological damage, I apologize.

"I couldn't wait," I tell them, hoping they'll turn away, "and now I can't stop. I'm peeing, that's all. It's nothing worth watching."

I cut through the whip-like leafless branches of the forsythia so I can stretch the fence through the brush, popping my head up to count the kids' heads—one, two, three. In the fading afternoon light, the sun over the treetops, cold air settles around me. Mittens and hats are strewn on the lawn, so I figure I ought to retrieve them and gauge fingers and ears. Collecting my tools, I head for the barn. What do I have to show for my time, for another day winding down? This fence I've been meaning to erect for two months now. Those fieldstones resting on the grass since summer wait to be pieced like a puzzle into the gravel path leading to the back door.

For all my lack of visible progress, my erratic behavior, sore back, and stiff joints, I want my children to see me as someone who's competent, strong, decisive; a person who fixes what's broken. To them I don't want to be a middle-aged man closing on fifty, but someone who knows what he's doing. Inside the barn, I dole out hammer, pliers, screwdriver, then squat on an overturned five-gallon bucket as they drop each tool into my toolbox. Justina delivers to me unbidden my level, disappears again. Apphia comes with a box wrench, Bea a square. I thank them as they pile the tools at my feet.

Soon supper will be ready, and afterward we'll head upstairs for baths. I'm tired, resentful of how much of my life they own, wondering how I keep going day after day.

I spot Justina, sequestered under my workbench, the top of her head a foot below the spruce planks. Bea tugs at my sleeve.

"Justina poop," she says.

"Thank you, Bea."

I leave the tools on the floor, go to stand, feel a snag in my lower back that makes me grab my side.

"Ouch," I say.

Then there's a gentle push upward against my elbow.

"I got you, Daddy," Bea tells me. "I got you."

Mokeeho

Priscilla Leigh McKinley

MY TWO-YEAR-OLD SON, JONATHAN, AND I sit on the couch in our living room, flipping through the pages of his Childcraft book about animals. I ask the questions and he answers. "What's this one?"

"Wetters, Mommy."

"Oh, letters." I flip to the next page. "What about this?"

"A mokeeho."

"Mokeeho? There's no such thing as a mokeeho," I laugh. "What is it?"

"Mokeeho," he repeats, scooting off the couch and running around the room, laughing. "Mokeehomokeeho."

Over the next several months, "Mokeeho" became Jonathan's imaginary friend. If we went shopping or to the park, Mokeeho was with us. If Jonathan got in trouble for something, Mokeeho was the culprit. Jonathan finally had a playmate, the brother or sister I would never be able to give him. But the significance of Mokeeho was much greater. Mokeeho reminded me that I might not be able to protect Jonathan the way other parents protect their children. Mokeeho reminded me that I was blind.

Mokeeho

Due to the complications of preeclampsia during my pregnancy and more than ten years with juvenile diabetes, I lost my sight on St. Patrick's Day, the day Jonathan was born. During the emergency C-section, the blood vessels in both of my eyes hemorrhaged, leaving me almost totally blind. Since I didn't have experience with either blindness or motherhood, the first few years of Jonathan's life were the most difficult of mine. I hadn't received enough training in blindness skills such as cane travel, so I refused to leave the apartment alone, fearing I would fall down a flight of stairs or get hit by a car. I worried I would be kidnapped or mugged or molested or, even worse, that something would happen to Jonathan. I was afraid of the mokeehos in the world, of what I couldn't see.

Jonathan and I lived in a lower level apartment, and I always kept the doors and windows locked, the curtains closed. Because I feared going outside, we spent the days watching game shows or playing in his room, often making robots and airplanes out of LEGOs while listening to Big Bird, Bert and Ernie, Oscar the Grouch, or Cookie Monster read books on tape. A cedar chest stood in front of the living room window and Jonathan would crawl up on it whenever he heard something outside. Since I wouldn't let him open the curtains, he would stand behind them, watching the neighborhood children play "Ring around the Rosy," "London Bridges," or kickball.

I only took Jonathan outside when I heard another mother out with her kids. I knew if something happened to Jonathan, the other mother would be able to see him. Cheryl, the mother of two girls, Ann and Mary, ages five and four, sat outside with her kids quite often. Mary was very quiet and enjoyed playing with Jonathan. Ann liked playing with

Jonathan, too, but for different reasons. She reminded me of Pippi Longstocking, sort of loud and obnoxious, running through the mud puddles in her sundresses and bare feet, never worrying about the dirt. For her, Jonathan, the youngest child in the apartment complex, was an easy target, someone she could bring to tears. If the kids played tag, Ann would make sure Jonathan was always it. If the kids jumped rope or played jacks, she would tell Jonathan he was too young to join them.

"You can't play, Jooooonnnnn," I overheard Ann say one day as I stood just inside the apartment door, her voice mean and whiny, stretching out the last syllable so it sounded like a fog horn.

"Why?" Jonathan cried, his voice shaking.

"'Cause I said so. I don't want you to play with us."

Jonathan cried louder. "But I wanna pway."

As soon as I flung open the door and stepped out on the sidewalk, Jonathan ran over to me and hugged my legs with his little arms, wiping his eyes and nose on my jeans. I looked in the direction of Ann's shadowy figure and gave her the blind evil eye.

"Come on, Jonathan. You don't want to play with someone mean." Then, scooping him up in my arms, I stepped back into the apartment and slammed the door as hard as I could.

As many times as I wanted to grab Ann and shake her, I was actually glad she was around. When Jonathan started begging to go out and play, she was the excuse I used for denying his requests. "Ann will just make you cry, so you might as well stay in." Then I would bribe him with a treat or a special video. Sometimes it worked. Other times, Jonathan insisted on going out. I guess he thought it would be better to be around mean kids than no kids at all.

I felt guilty for not letting Jonathan be a "normal" kid, but, at the time, I didn't know what else to do. I didn't think of the parents I had seen in Kmart, frantically running through the aisles, calling out the names of their lost children. I thought I was the only mother who worried about protecting her child. I didn't know how a blind person could keep a child safe. How could I tell if he ran out in front of a car? How could I keep him from going down big slides, from climbing trees, from being a kid? I didn't want to smother him, but what could I do? I wanted him to have a normal childhood, to experiment, to learn, to grow, but how could I give him that freedom and still be assured of his safety?

A month before Jonathan's second birthday, he and I went to the store to get groceries. The store was only about five blocks from our house, but I was afraid to walk that far, especially in the snow, so we took the bus, which stopped about half a block from our apartment. Jonathan and I had been to the store several times, and I had memorized the items in each aisle, so I could usually tell when we were nearing the canned vegetables or the frozen pizzas. As I pushed the cart through the aisles, Jonathan picked out the items we needed. He could not talk very well, yet he could understand what I wanted when I told him to "get the one Mommy uses." If we were in the cleaning-supply section, Jonathan would grab a bottle of Era from the shelf; if we were in the dairy section, he would grab a box of Parkay. If the store moved things around, Jonathan and I threw fits, mine a little quieter than his. That posed the only problem, except for the boxes of Twinkies and Ding Dongs I often found when unpacking the groceries at home.

On this particular day, when Jonathan and I reached the front of the store to pay, there were lines at every register, and it took much longer than expected. As we were leaving the store, Jonathan let me know the bus was pulling away from the stop. "B's! B's!" he shrieked. With my cane in one hand and Jonathan's hand in the other, two full plastic bags of groceries hanging from my arms, we hurried outside. Jonathan pulled me through the icy parking lot, but it was too late. I could hear the bus pulling out into the heavy traffic, the sound disappearing down the street. Jonathan started screaming. I yelled at him to stop. Then I threw down the bags of groceries, sat down in a snow bank, and cried. I didn't know how we would make it home. I didn't know what to do. When I got up and told Jonathan we had to walk, he screamed even louder. He wanted me to carry him, but, already weighed down with the bags of groceries and my cane, it was physically impossible. So, with Jonathan leading the way through the crusty snow, we walked home, teardrops freezing to our faces.

I had a red corduroy vest/leash for Jonathan, sort of like a guide dog's harness, but I only used it once. I was afraid someone would cut the cord without my knowledge, just as another cord had been cut months before. Then, unconscious on the operating room table, I was unaware of what was happening to me, unaware that at the moment the umbilical cord was being cut, the blood vessels in my eyes were hemorrhaging. No, I couldn't take the chance that someone might take Jonathan, leaving me with nothing but a bright red corduroy cord hanging limply from my hand. Instead, I depended on Jonathan to lead me around by the hand, sometimes crying because he wanted me to carry him, wanted me to do the leading, wanted me to be like the other mothers he saw in the neighborhood. I depended on him to tell me when cars were coming, when it was safe to cross the street. I depended on him to do what I was supposed to be doing—protecting.

One year after Mokeeho's entrance into our lives, Jonathan and I are again going through his Childcraft book about animals.

"What's this?" I ask.

"A mosquito," he says clearly.

Laughing and then beginning to cry, I hold my face in my hands. Jonathan doesn't remember how he got his imaginary friend, Mokeeho. He doesn't remember that I told him there's no such thing as a mokeeho. The realization that Jonathan knew the answer and I told him he was wrong hurts. But I also know that in spite of my blindness, Jonathan is learning. In spite of all the mokeehos in the world, Jonathan is going to be fine.

"Why are you crying, Mommy?" Jonathan asks, putting his hand on my teary cheek.

I pull my hands away from my face and smile. "I'm not crying, Jonathan. Even though I can't see it, I know you're right. It's a mosquito."

Why Does Your Son Have a Phallus on His Head?

Jennifer Margulis

BELLIES PROTRUDING, we stood in a circle practicing sounds, exhaling and moaning as we lowered our arms onto our swollen abdomens. "Now say 'MAH,'" the instructor guided us. "'MAH,' like mama, is a comforting sound."

I had had no trouble with the "OH"—imagining the cervix ohpening up; I liked the "UM"—it reminded me of the Buddhist chanting and the smell of sandalwood that used to come from my former housemate's room as she performed her nightly rituals; but when I tried to say "MAH" my mouth twisted awkwardly and my breath stuck in my throat. I left the prenatal yoga class early that day, cried with the abandon of a woman eight months pregnant, and never returned.

I cannot remember any time when "mama" was a comforting sound. Although my mother breast-fed me for four months, she then returned to her world of the microcosm and her lab at Boston University, and left me in the care of various nannies—all of whom I remember well. There was Abi, who watched me when I was an infant and a toddler. Her olive skin smelled of chocolate and her hugs were warm and sweaty. Claudette could balance five telephone books on her head while dancing; she unbuttoned her pants after she ate to let her tummy air; and she was always ready with a broad smile and loud laugh, even after she sent Regine, her daughter, back to Haiti because she could not afford to keep her in the States. Then for a brief time came a woman with pasty skin and clipped speech who would not let us eat cake after she baked it (because it had to cool) and who forbade us from playing in our room after she had cleaned it (because we might mess it up). And finally Denise, a friend of Claudette's, who was there watching soap operas when Zach and I tore home from school (the rule in our house was no television until four o'clock, but Denise never minded if we sat with her). Denise did the housework and barely spoke. She was a solid presence, but no laughter filled our house like it had when Claudette lived with us.

In nursery school there was a teacher whom I adored. She had long light-brown hair and wore thick glasses like my mother. Unlike my mother, she sang to me and hugged me and listened to me and told me things. She put her glasses over her hair and pretended to be a monster. She was tall and beautiful and her long hair and big earrings were like my Aunt Judy's. If she weren't my real mother, I decided when I was three, then my real mother was very much like her. My father insisted he had been in the room when I was born, but I knew I was adopted. I had a real mother somewhere who loved me. Not an absent mother whom I almost never saw, whose nearsighted eyes barely focused on me, who did not seem to notice that she had four children—three sons and a daughter.

The moment my daughter was born, my mother, who sat in the labor room correcting a manuscript, announced that Hesperus was just like me. With her sticky-outy ears and her long crinkled eyelashes, Hesperus looked so exactly like her father that I thought at first she was a boy. "She's a di Properzio," my mother said, "but she's just like you were. She's all James in looks and all you in every other way." As Hesperus's skinny froglike legs turned into fat pudgy thighs, and as I noticed that maybe something about her eyes looked just a little bit like me, I wondered if my mother was right, if in my daughter I could see something of myself.

I slept wrapped around her tiny body, addicted to her sweet smell and infuriated, almost hysterical, when my mother-in-law's perfume rubbed off on my baby. I nursed her while blisters formed on my nipples and while she sucked off the scabs that came after. James and I wrote long love letters to her detailing her birth, her alert eyes, and her strong muscle tone in a journal we called "Dear Chickpea" (because once she had been that small).

When Hesperus was three days old it took three of us—my husband, my best-friend Sue, and me—to change her. We had her bare legs cocked above her head when we heard a low rumble. Then a spray of poop shot over the changing table and landed on the adjacent bookcase, fanning out like buckshot to befoul two shelves of my work-related research books. Our red-faced baby grunted in relief as we scrambled to cover her with a clean diaper. I realized even then that Hesperus was asserting her primacy in my life.

I went back to work full time when she was six weeks old, teaching literature classes on Tuesdays and Thursdays, putting an

Why Does Your Son Have a Phallus on His Head?

"Exam in Progress" sign on the door of my tiny office every three hours and pumping breast milk into plastic bottles. Instead of feeling relieved to be out of the house, and despite my success at my job, I found myself missing my little girl, worrying that her childhood was slipping by without me.

When Hesperus was ten months old a job brought us from the New South to New England, closer to my mother's orbit. At every visit to our house my mother would denigrate her mothering abilities and remark that she liked being a grandmother much more than she had ever liked being a mother, that she was glad to hand the baby back. Hesperus, though, adored her. She liked the gold pendant my mother wore around her neck (a hunter case watch, set fast): at a year she liked to pull on it and bite it, at two she would sit on her grandmother's lap and work at opening the locket. She was fascinated by my mother's dog, an overweight mongrel known to the police and the pound for his frequent visits to both, thought by most in the small college town where my mother lives to be a stray (my mother's idea of taking Roosevelt for a walk is to let him off the leash to forage in garbage cans and battle skunks). Hesperus often asked, "Where Grandma Lynnie go?"

"I think she's at work," I answered.

We threw a toddler party for Halloween and invited my mother. Hesperus wobbled around the house in a green elf costume, the pointy hat on her head a perfect complement to her own pointy ears. Before the trick-or-treating she and her friends—a panther, a tiger, Spiderman, and an elephant—chased each other around in circles, in and out of rooms, doorways, and halls. Quin, in orange Spiderman pajamas that were already too small, sped ahead. Hesperus followed after, momentarily alone in the hallway. When she finally caught up to him she dissolved into laughter, doubled over with delight at Quin's reappearance. Then off Quin went again and Hesperus followed, suddenly serious and silent, her whole self bent on catching him.

When Grandma Lynnie finally arrived, two hours late, apologizing, enthusing, and flossing her teeth, we were lining the toddlers up for pictures. Without introducing herself to his parents, my mother pointed at P. J. in his gray elephant outfit. "Why," she asked, "does your son have a phallus on his head?"

When the weather finally warmed Hesperus and I walked together along a nature path that follows Fort River. Her bare feet pitter pattered alongside the empty stroller I pushed (that she refused to sit in). She crouched to examine a leaf, ran forward to an exposed root, and then rushed back to me.

After a few more steps she stopped and shrieked horribly. She had stepped on a thorny branch.

I sat her in the stroller and held her leg tightly to remove the thorn from the bottom of her foot. She howled. Blood streamed out. Then Hesperus stopped crying abruptly. "Juice!" she exclaimed, smiling as she watched the bright red liquid leave her body.

In another minute she demanded to get out of the stroller. But the bottom of her foot was tender and she did not want to walk. I hoisted her onto my shoulders.

For two minutes she enjoyed reaching up and knocking the rain off tall tree leaves.

Why Does Your Son Have a Phallus on His Head?

"Get down! Get down! Get down!" she screamed.

I put her down.

"Carry you! Carry you!"

I picked her up.

"NO! Not on shoulders!" My patience, which had been steadily running out, grain by grain as if from an hourglass, was gone. In the middle of the still woods I yelled things I instantly regretted in a tone of voice uglier than I knew myself capable of. Then I sat on the wet ground and held my head in my hands. Hesperus put out her little arms to me. She rested her head on my shoulder, "Mommy sad. Mommy say?" and patted my back. We sang songs and I told her stories about Charlie, an elephant whose antics—getting stuck in blackberry brambles and finding a bed big enough to sleep in— sparked her imagination.

"No car! No car!" she screamed when we got back to the car.

She cried the entire way home. Her eyes puffed and reddened and tears made wet tracks down her face.

Sometimes two-year-old Hesperus reminds me of my mother. They share an intense curiosity about the world, a fascination with small things and dangerous objects; they are both energetic to a fault; they both get up early and aspire to go to bed late; they are frank about body parts; they love to be outdoors, to read, and to talk. I see in Hesperus little flashes of her grandmother's genius. As she runs around the house stark naked ("Nudie petutie!") I admire the curve of her legs and her strong back and I realize that those legs are my legs, and that I got them from my mother.

Some days Hesperus is full of frenetic energy, whirling from one danger to the next. Her eye barely misses the sharp corner of a table; she wrestles an empty laundry basket and heaves it toward me; she takes off for someplace and trips on a wrinkle in the carpet, or on her feet, or on nothing at all. When Hesperus reminds me of my midwife's two-year-old son who squeezed five baby chicks to death before his parents realized he was holding them too tightly, who wields a broom over his head and shoves his toy cow hard into my daughter's trusting face, I sense that her flightiness is her way of communicating through behavior what she does not yet have the words to express. Something is wrong—maybe she is tired or hungry or worried—but she does not know what the problem is, or how to fix it.

When she skins her knee on the smooth carpet she is asking me to help her, to stop her from hurting herself, to feed her, perhaps, or to put her to bed. I can scoop my daughter up in my arms and march her upstairs, Blue Blue Blankie slung over her shoulders. I can truncate her bedtime ritual—one book instead of two, nummies, teeth brushing, only the French version of "Frère Jacques"—and put her to sleep.

Like Hesperus, my mother is often frantic. At her house the phone rings constantly, the dog barks himself hoarse, classical music blares from five different radios, each clock shows a different time, all fast. My mother eats standing up, seldom says hello or good-bye, talks too loudly and interrupts constantly. She reads voraciously at night, Chomsky, Dickinson, Wittgenstein, but cannot relinquish the day to sleep. Instead she dozes propped up with the book in her hand, loses her grasp so that the book hits her in the face and wakes her, rousing her to read another paragraph.

Why Does Your Son Have a Phallus on His Head?

I try to help my mother too—I make her tea, invite her to sit down and relax, ask her about her day. I study her face that, at sixty-three, radiates energy and beauty, and notice her graying hair and worry lines, lines that I would like to smooth away. But I have never been an effective mother to her, as much as I tried when I was little. The only time I have seen her unhurried was when she had an internal hemorrhage and lost half her body's blood. Hooked up to an IV and a respirator, my mother stayed still. My brother, Zach, drove from New York, I speeded from Boston, and we met at the hospital. But even then she was out of my reach. Although I could take care of the details—contacting her publisher about a book cover, phoning her lover in Barcelona, negotiating the delivery of a new dresser, meeting with a lawyer to draft legal documents to make me her health-care proxy—I could not heal her.

"I never was a good nurse," my mother said, holding my hand for a moment. "I have no patience for sick people."

The last time my mother came over for dinner she helped me get Hesperus ready for bed. Drying Hesperus off with a bath towel, my mother tickled her feet and played coochy-coo with her. For the first time in my daughter's life her grandmother made her giggle. Then the three of us lay on the bed together ("Cozy cozy!") and my mother read us *Madeline.* As soon as the story was finished, Hesperus pleaded, "More that book again, Grandma Lynnie!" My mother ignored her. Instead, she reached for the telephone to call the answering machine at her lab for messages.

The Tea Party

Samuel P. Clark

USUALLY IT HAPPENS when I've just stretched out on the couch. I've kicked off my shoes, adjusted the cushions, and hoped for a little mindless channel-surfing or even a cocktail-hour snooze, when my two-year-old daughter comes bounding around any of several corners and bounces up against the sofa. Her small, bopping vertical head face-to-face with my wanna-be-lazy horizontal one, she poses the question: "Go in Kayla's room?"

Now, when Kayla does this, her voice is a song of soft gentility, but—make no mistake—the effect is the same as if a big burly police officer had just approached my vehicle and said, "Sir, do you mind stepping out of your car?" My compliance is certain—it's just a question of how difficult I want to make it for myself.

Kayla has a repertoire that ranges from repeating this offer as slow, methodical torture, emphasizing all the Os, as in "Want tooooo goooo in Kayla's rooom?" to spitting it out like bullets from a semi-automatic weapon, barely pausing for breath and losing some of the less meaningful words: "Wanna go Kayla's room wanna go Kayla's room wanna go Kayla's room?"

The Tea Party

Whatever selection she has made for the first round, it is often followed with, "Want come with me?" The urgency of this query is emphasized with a finger-grab. The translation here is (Officer to Mr. Clark): "Sir, you can come quietly or we can do it another way, but I'm taking this finger down to the station." Mr. Clark to Kayla: "I'd love to come, just please let Daddy have his pinkie back. It's not supposed to be as big as Tall Man."

When we get to Kayla's doorway, she announces, "Kayla's room is messy, messy, messy." I guess this is a two-year-old's variation on the familiar "I've been on my feet all day and haven't had a second to clean." I'm a guest in this room, and being forewarned means I'm fore-armed as I gingerly sweep away puzzles, teddy bears, books, and plastic barnyard animals to clear a place to squat.

For a moment we just sit there, cross-legged, viewing each other and considering our surroundings, happy to be together. Then she finds things to do. Play with the castle, put pennies between her toes, and so forth. I like these games with her, biding our time until she says, "Want have tea, Daddy?"

"Yes, please. That would be wonderful."

I bought Kayla a little tea set while on a business trip when she was about eighteen months old. I figured it was something she and her mom might enjoy when Kayla reached around age four or five, and that, perhaps, I too might be invited for a cup now and again. Well, the present was opened as soon as I showed it to her mother, and we've been having tea parties ever since.

It's a strawberry-themed set. The thimble-sized cups are red, spotted with tiny yellow seeds, and the handles are brown stems adorned with delicate green leaves. In the original display, there were cups and saucers, a sugar bowl, a cream pitcher, and, of course, a teapot. Today, amid all the clutter, it is impossible, as it is at most parties, to find all the original and proper china. So Kayla, a good hostess, and I, a polite guest, look for ways to make do.

"Ah, Kayla, I found the teapot inside your shoe." She is pleased. "Look, Daddy. Here a cup," she chirps as she unsettles a stuffed rabbit perched against the wall. And so it goes as we slowly set our table.

We decide that half a plastic Easter egg makes a fine second teacup, and, for the sugar bowl, we use a hippopotamus bottom from one of those find-a-hippo-in-yet-another-hippo puzzles. I explain to her that hippopotamuses have big cellulite bottoms anyway, so a bit of extra sugar shouldn't matter. It's obvious she doesn't really get it, but I'll punish her with my humor all her life, just like I do her mom. We decide that the milk bottle that came with her baby doll will work perfectly for cream. Kayla offers me an air cookie from a puzzle piece resembling some part of Big Bird's anatomy.

"Oh, Kayla, these cookies are delicious. Do you want to try one?" She does and takes an air bite.

"Want some tea, Daddy?"

"Yes, please." I raise my egg (I've allowed her the real strawberry cup).

"May I offer you some sugar, Kayla?"

"Yes, pweez."

I dig into the hippo bottom with a plastic fork and aim it over Kayla's cup. "Another?"

"Yes, pweez."

I bring forth a heaping mound of invisible sugar and stir it in Kayla's cup as she adds cream to mine from the toy bottle. Now, with everything prepared, we cradle our cups carefully in our hands, ready to drink.

"Remember to blow, Kayla, it might be hot."

She takes a sip and says, "Daddy, my tea is tasty and sweet."

As I put the cup to my mouth, my small hostess watches patiently but expectantly for my verdict. Smacking my lips, I exclaim, "Mmm, Kayla, mine is too. May I have some more?"

Her smile fills my heart as she refills my cup.

Big Bird Is Just Big Bird

Eve S. Weinbaum

MY CHILD THINKS I'M A BOY. I realized this when we were reading a story one day and Jonah pointed to a picture of a little boy and said, "Who is that?" I wasn't sure what he was asking, but I thought maybe he recognized a child similar to himself in the book's illustration, so I said, "It looks like Jonah."

He said "noooo" in that tone of voice that suggests he is sorry I am slightly feeble-minded. "It's not Jonah, it's Mommy!"

I asked him, "Is Mommy a little boy?"

"Noooo . . . " he said again. "Mommy is a BIG boy."

It surprises me, not because I expect two-year-old Jonah to understand sex or gender, but because he is so expert at differentiation. He can tell a crow from a parrot from an owl from a kingfisher. He would never misidentify a dump truck, bulldozer, steam shovel, jeep, or tractor. He knows the difference between daffodils, tulips, daisies, and black-eyed Susans. He remembers the names and relationships of all his friends and family, knows that Aviva is his little sister, that Mommy's mommy is called Bubby, that Isabel's daddy is

Steve. But ask him to identify categories of people and he is utterly confounded. We look at a drawing of several people and I ask him which one looks like his friend Charlotte. He chooses a small dark Asian boy. (Charlotte has ivory skin and white-blond hair.) I ask which picture looks like his grandfather Gralex, thinking Jonah will choose the man with the gray beard. Jonah chooses an African-American girl jumping rope.

When it comes to identifying people, Jonah's brain seems to focus upon an entirely different set of characteristics. He doesn't look at the things that seem most obvious to me: hair color, size, skin tone, or clothing. Instead, it seems he tries to size up the person's character or personality. And when people's looks change, Jonah is unfazed. When I recently cut off all my long hair, I feared that my two toddlers would wonder what had happened to their mommy. Since I know that preschoolers often equate very short hair with masculinity, I expected both of my children to be surprised or agitated, at least momentarily. But neither child even seemed to notice the change. Finally, I brought it up. Jonah wanted to know if the barber had given me a lollipop (why else would anyone submit to a haircut?). I told him I had received no lollipop, and he never gave my short hair a second thought.

At an art gallery recently, Jonah was commenting on all the pictures and identifying the images he recognized: "Look Mommy, a cow!" he would exclaim, or "Is that your favorite kind of butterfly?!" When we came to an exhibit that included many large portraits of nude women, I wondered what Jonah would say. I had considered skipping that room and distracting him with the promise of an ice-cream treat. But

I decided not to be that uptight—so what if we had to discuss pubic hair in loud exclamatory tones with sophisticated art patrons nearby?—and we stood there examining the sensual drawings. Jonah looked interested. He watched me look at the pictures. I could see that something was bothering him about the art, and I wondered what he would say about his first exposure to so many naked ladies. He's mildly obsessed with his own body parts, and I expected him to comment on bodies so different from his. Finally he figured out what was disturbing him about the images: "Mommy, that man has no shirt!"

I'm not sure what two-year-olds have to tell us about gender, but I know that it's not what the experts think. In a recent bag of hand-me-downs I found my sister-in-law's copy of *What to Expect in the First Year* and I read a discussion of sex roles in the question-and-answer section. "No matter how we try," the mythical parents query the experts, "we can't induce our eleven-month-old son to be nurturing with dolls—he prefers to throw them against a wall." The authors reassure the anxious couple that not only is their child's behavior normal, it is absolutely unavoidable. "Sexual sameness is an ideal whose time can never come—at least as long as Mother Nature continues to have some say in the matter. Boys and girls are, for the most part, molded in the womb, not in the playroom and backyard. . . . Remember the fact that there are innate differences between males and females." The book enumerates some of these differences: "Boys are much more aggressive both physically and verbally, while girls are more compliant. Boys come to like group play, girls one-on-one."

Big Bird Is Just Big Bird

No one told this to my toddlers. They and their daycare friends violate willy-nilly the rules laid out in this modern-day bible of parenting. The three girls are fearless and loud, even aggressive at times, and they boss around a happily obedient little Jonah. Jonah's one-year-old sister, Aviva, has never met playground equipment she didn't love, no matter how treacherous, and nothing makes her happier than very loud trucks and buses. She hits when she gets frustrated, refuses to hold hands in traffic, and terrorizes the neighbors' pets. Jonah is nervous in more than two inches of water, hates to be pushed high on the swings, and gets upset at the sound of a lawnmower. He began speaking at an earlier age than Aviva, has endless patience for arts and crafts, and loves to listen quietly to stories for hours at a time—while his sister, after two pages of her favorite book, climbs down to run around, yell, and tumble. In our house, Aviva is more likely to be the one testing the rules and slamming the dolls around, while Jonah likes to wrap them up in blankets and sing lullabies to them. Not that I expect these particular personality traits to last—any parent of toddlers knows better than to think any behavior, good or bad, will remain constant from one week to the next. But I can see why toddlers don't intuitively understand the gender roles that the rest of the world believes to be so obvious.

Last night as I was putting Jonah to bed, he snuggled under his blue blanket and hugged his best friend, Big Bird. He showed me all the new tricks he had taught Big Bird recently, like how to shake his head yes and no, do somersaults, and sing "This Old Man." I had gender on my mind, so I asked Jonah if Big Bird was a girl or a boy. The answer was clear: "No, Mommy. He's just Big Bird."

Pretender to the Throne

Geoff Griffin

It's not like I come in here for a break. I always hurry to get done and back out before my two-year-old daughter has time to harm herself. I took every precaution before coming in here. I made sure the front door was locked, the stove wasn't on. I even turned on cartoons to keep her distracted.

But as it turns out all my work was for nothing. I've only been gone a few seconds when I hear my daughter coming to look for me.

"Dad, where are you?"

"I'm in here, honey."

I want her to be reassured and know that I'm in the house, but I don't want her to know exactly where I am. I just need two uninterrupted minutes to sit down here and figure out what we are going to do with the rest of this day.

It seems like we've already done everything there is to do. We've played plenty of horsy. I've had all the hide-and-seek I can handle for one day. We've colored entire coloring books. We've read the same stories through so many times that I can quote *The Cat in the Hat* and other entire kids' books verbatim. Playing with stuffed animals? Done it—twice.

To top it off, it's raining hard, so a walk to the park or the library is out of the question. How am I going to get her through the day?

"Dad, where are you?"

My daughter is a relentless pursuer.

"I'm in here, honey."

She keeps doing this until she gets closer and closer and eventually tracks me down.

I've left the door slightly ajar, just to make sure I can hear everything that's going on out there. She comes walking in and says, "Why are you sitting down?"

"I'm going potty, sweetie."

"Why?"

She's still in diapers.

"Well, because I needed to go."

"Oh."

Now that we've got that settled, she isn't prepared to leave. She starts looking around.

"Why don't you go back out and watch some cartoons? I'll be right back out."

This doesn't elicit much of a response—mainly because she is looking around the adults' bathroom for new things to play with.

She finds the toilet brush and picks it up. She starts swinging it around.

"Put that back down. That's not something to play with."

"Why?"

"Because it's very dirty. It's what we use to clean the toilet."

"Why?"

"Because toilets get dirty and we have to clean them."

She puts the brush back down and starts looking elsewhere to see what she can find.

"Why don't you go and watch cartoons and I'll be out in just a minute."

"Dad, I'm hungry," she says while opening and closing one of the cabinet drawers to see how it works.

"You had a snack just a half-hour ago."

"I'm hungry."

"Okay, I'll make you another snack after I'm done in here."

"I'm hungry."

"I know, but I can't make you a snack until I'm done in here." I realize my voice is rising. I take it back down a level. "You need to go watch cartoons and in just a minute I'll come out and make you a snack."

"When?"

"As soon as I'm done in here."

"When?"

"In just a minute. Once you get back out there you'll hardly notice any time has passed before I'm there with your snack."

This is a flat-out lie. There is no slower passing of time in the world than when a toddler is waiting for something. "One minute"—I might as well say one month—but I'm getting pretty desperate here.

I'm hoping she'll get going when I glance around to see she's found the soap in the shower.

"Soap!" she says as she holds it up proudly.

"You're right. That's soap, but that's Mommy and Daddy's soap, so you need to put it back."

She looks disappointed, but does as I say.

Once she puts the soap down she looks at the ground and discovers the floor mat. She wraps it around her shoulders and lifts her arms up and down.

"Look, Daddy, I'm a butterfly!"

"Yes, you're a very beautiful butterfly, but you need to put that down."

"But I want to be a butterfly."

There's no reason she can't keep doing that. It wouldn't really hurt anything. Maybe it would even get her out of here.

"Why don't you go flying around the house?" I offer hopefully, but her attention has already been diverted. She drops the floor mat and goes to inspect the can of shaving cream.

"What's this?"

"That's Daddy's shaving cream."

"The stuff that makes you look like Santa?"

"Yes."

Hey, here's my chance.

"Look, I'll put a little bit on your face so you can look like Santa."

I squirt out a little bit of the white foam and dab it on her face.

"Now run into your room and look in the mirror to see what it looks like!"

"I can see here," she says, pointing to the mirror above the sink.

She starts to climb up onto the sink to look in the mirror but it turns out badly. She slips and falls and starts crying.

It's clear that I'm not going to accomplish the task I came here for so I stand quickly, pull my trousers up, and start washing my hands as fast as I can so that I can pick her up.

"Did you go potty, Daddy?" my daughter asks.

One o'clock seems agonizingly far away.

Willful Girl

Nicole Cooley

WHEN THE AMNIOCENTESIS REVEALED that our baby would be a
girl, I began to imagine it: my daughter and I curled up together in
our four-poster bed, wearing long nightgowns, a circle of dusky rose
lamplight illuminating the book in my hands. I read, she turned the
pages, we leaned our heads close, our long hair touching. The book,
of course, was *Little Women*, my childhood favorite. For the rest of
that summer of my last trimester, I pictured my daughter. She'd be
pale, slender, and dark-haired. She'd look like the color illustrations
of Beth, my secret favorite sister from the book. But while Beth dies
midway through Alcott's novel, my daughter would thrive, a delicate yet lush blossom. The middle name we'd chosen for her—Iris,
the name of my favorite flower—would suit her perfectly.

This Louisa May Alcott fantasy stemmed from my own childhood. Among my happiest early memories are ones of my mother
reading to me, for hours, first from Little Golden Books, then from
the classics that centered on the lives of girls: *The Secret Garden, The
Little Princess,* and, most of all, *Little Women.* My mother always did
the voices, and she read with great expression. If I loved a book, she

would make me an outfit from it on her sewing machine. My sister and I had Laura Ingalls Wilder bonnets and aprons. I was frequently sick with pneumonia as a child, and my mother made me a pink calico nightgown like Beth's. Those moments—when my mother held me close, arm crooked over my shoulder, and read to me into the night—made me love books, made me want to write them. And they defined for me what the mother-daughter relationship, at its best, would be.

The day Meridian was born, weighing in at nine pounds two ounces, with almost no hair, a round face, and cobalt blue eyes that I felt could stare right through me, she immediately proved herself to be the opposite of Beth. She looks exactly like my husband and nothing like me. I've even been asked by strangers on the streets of our New York City neighborhood if I am her baby-sitter.

At fifteen months, Meridian is a lively, exuberant little girl who bears absolutely no resemblance to my Louisa May Alcott fantasy. She loves to be read to and to "read" on her own and owns more books than most adults. She can push a chair across the room by herself. At thirty pounds and thirty-two inches, she is beautiful, robust, hardly ever sick, and she is, as my grandmother would say, "a pistol."

"Well, she's willful," the pediatrician says at her check-up, as he examines her ears, though I can barely make out his words over Meridian's screams and can concentrate on nothing but soothing this child—cheeks flushed red from anger, mouth open in an enormous howl—and trying to prevent her from hitting him in the face. "And she's going to get more so."

All the way back on the subway, while my husband holds her on his lap and reads to her to calm her down, I turn the word over and over in my mind. I ask my husband, "Don't you think it's *good* for a girl to be willful? Don't we want her to be tough?"

In fact, her willfulness becomes more and more evident each day. When my husband lifts her up from our bed at 5:00 A.M., her customary wake-up hour, she sobs as if her heart would break if I sleep on till seven o'clock without her. Little tears pour down her cheeks and her fists strike the air in fury if I set her down for a minute to put on my coat after I've promised we're going outside to see birds.

"Let's go get a clean diaper." I pick her up and head for the changing table in our bedroom.

"No!" She looks me straight in the eye. "No!" Once I manage to settle her in position, she demands a book. Not a silly baby board book but the book I'm currently reading, Dan Savage's story of gay adoption, *The Kid,* which is splayed open on the nearby table. As I unfasten her diaper, she flips the pages, studying the words, her expression serious, her brow slightly furrowed: the exact expression my husband has when he reads.

Sometimes when I watch her clap her doll's hands or dance to "Pop Goes the Weasel" or toddle around the living room crashing into the sofa and the wing chair, I remember what happened at the hospital right after she was born. After the birth, a difficult emergency C-section, she was taken to the nursery. No one brought her to us. A few hours later, two neonatologists came to my room to tell us they thought there was something wrong with our daughter. Through my nausea and morphine haze, I heard them say they were worried about her brain, they wanted to do an MRI immediately, and they needed our signed permission to sedate her. My husband signed a form, then went into the bathroom to cry. For the rest of the morning we waited in agony for someone to bring our baby back. I bargained with a God I was struggling to believe in: I swore I'd be less selfish, I'd be nicer, I'd take my job less seriously and remember what was most important, my child, as long as she was okay. At noon, Meridian was wheeled into the room in her glass bassinet, and we were told she was fine. But the next day it happened again: this time she was taken away to have an EKG and an echocardiogram by doctors concerned about a possible heart defect. Again, she was gone for hours, and then we were told nothing was wrong. Both times, the doctors in charge were nonchalant when they wheeled her back in her baby Isolette chamber.

When I look at her now, I can still recall the feelings of that waiting. I can feel the pressure of the air in my room high above the East River, which shined silver in the winter light. I remember how I ached to just hold my new baby like all the other mothers on the maternity floor, to smooth her pink skin, to press my lips to hers. My husband and I never had those after-birth moments we had been told about in our birthing classes. Five days later, when we finally left the hospital, as I held her swaddled on my lap in the wheelchair, I could not stop crying. As we rode out through the lobby, strangers smiled at the vision of mother and baby going home, mother overcome with joy. But I cried because I had gotten a small inkling of what it would be like to lose my baby, and I vowed to never let her go.

Now when my daughter spins on the living room rug, refuses to sleep, won't stay in her stroller, over and over I am thankful for her exuberance. I kiss her belly and call her my Riot Grrrl, my tough chick, my little drama queen. On the couch, she slaps her hand on the pages of her Mother Goose book to tell me which nursery rhyme to read. I hold her as tight and close as I can till she spills from my lap, wriggles out of my arms to play.

Now I can't imagine her wearing that pink calico nightgown. As Meridian approaches her second birthday, I know that she's not Beth, she's not me, she's her own new girl, and just as I know this I finally let go of my own childhood to look forward into our future.

Willy Walks

Joyce Maynard

THE DAY WILLY TOOK HIS FIRST STEP our whole life changed. Now he climbs stairs and teeters at the top with one foot poised in midair. Now when his older brother and sister play Candy Land, he can stand in the middle of the game board, throwing cards in the air. He pulls ingredients off shelves, he makes Cheerios mountains and pours olive oil on his head. He wakes up, shouting, at half-past five—ready to start his endless investigation of our decimated house ("What shall I break?" were the first words he uttered one morning.) He goes to bed at eight-thirty, and Steve and I follow as soon after that as possible. We drop into bed every night with heavy sighs. "Three children is a lot," says Steve.

I wanted three children, and maybe more. Of course I can't imagine doing without any one of them. It's just that right now, life around here is so grueling I have to make advance arrangements just to step into the bathroom.

I lie awake, projecting into our future. In two years, Willy will be the age that Charlie is now—almost three (an age that seems thrillingly mature and independent by comparison). Someday, I murmur to Steve, we will have a three-year-old, a five-year-old, and a nine-year-old. Someday they will be five, seven, and eleven. Six, eight, and twelve . . . I spin the different combinations in my head like a gambler, dreaming of the perfect hand.

I call up a friend who has a child a few months older than Willy (I dial twice, because the first time my son pulls my glasses off. As we talk, he sings into the receiver, which is wet where he licked it. He grabs for my coffee. Points at the record player, demanding music. Gets himself tangled up in my extra-long telephone cord). "How long does this stage last?" I ask her. "When does it get easier?"

"Search me," she says. "I'm still waiting."

Our older two children are taking the new Willy surprisingly well, considering. They're devoted to him, even though (in the last two days) he has destroyed three pop-up books, the right paw of a Gremlin puzzle, and one of Mr. T's ears. Where once my children used to beg me to play cards or blocks, now all they can hope for, often, is that I'll get their brother out of their hair. "Mo-om!" they call out, at least thirty times a day. "Come get Will."

But he doesn't want me, of course. He's a wriggler, not a cuddler, and what he really wants are the other kids. He's a third child: the one I had no time to nurse after the fourth month. The one who got his milk unheated, straight from the refrigerator.

Willy's the one we were always calling by his brother's name (it had been so recently that we'd had that other blond-haired baby boy under our roof). He's the one we never got around to sending out announcements about, never took pictures of. He grew, like one of those weeds that somehow manage to push up through the cracks in a sidewalk, without a whole lot of close tending. Of course he walked at ten months: He could see this was no house to be a baby in. Not this year, anyway. Better to get moving, to grow up fast. So he did, and he has.

Our third child is a wonderful, cheerful baby, who smiles when his brother bops him on the head with a stuffed animal. Once when he was a few months old I heard a loud noise upstairs, where he was napping, followed by a small peep. I couldn't go check it out right away because Charlie had just got stuck in the sofa, while Audrey was trying to fold up the hideaway bed with him inside, and somebody had turned on the hot-air popcorn popper without putting a bowl underneath to catch the popcorn. When I finally managed to investigate upstairs, I discovered the bottom had fallen out of Willy's crib (which is, like everything else he uses, pretty beat up, from the two previous occupants). He was lying on the floor with his mattress on his head, cooing.

I tell these stories to friends, who smile ruefully, but they're sad stories too. I love babies, love sitting in a chair, just rocking them, smelling the tops of their heads, studying their toes, and I haven't gotten to do those things much this time around. Not that Willy's suffering: he has a brother who (in spite of the occasional bop) almost never races through a room without stopping to pat his head, and a sister who likes to hold him by the armpits and waltz him around the room to our Cyndi Lauper record.

Mostly I'm sad for Steve and me, that we're seldom able to relish this time and take it slow, that all we can do right now is grit our teeth and count the months until it's over and we don't have a baby around here anymore. And then—oh, will we ever miss it.

Slow to Warm

Brett Paesel

It's a dream. I know this because the moonlight hits the water like it's in a cheap motel painting. My two-year-old son walks along the edge of a pier, naked, wobbling impossibly on the drop-off. I follow him, covered in layers and layers of clothing. I think, *Wow, this is weird.* It's weird in the way that twice-baked potatoes or pretzel salad are weird. But I'm not too fazed. I know that this is a dream, for Christ's sake, and it could get a whole lot weirder. In seconds I could be eating my contact lenses, which is a recurring thing with me.

Suddenly, Spence dives into the water. I stop. Every cell of my body electric. My heart thumps fast and my eyes lock onto his watery form. He kicks his legs, but doesn't rise to the top.

I have to jump in. I start removing layers of clothing. I think, *I've got to get these clothes off, so I don't drag him down.* At the same time I know that I shouldn't bother with the goddamned clothes. I should just jump in, for God's sake. But I can't. I've got to get these clothes off, and I rip them—tearing them off me as I keep my eyes fixed on Spence, who sinks farther down.

Then I think, *Wait! I can stop this. I can just stop the dream.* I force my mind through some thick cosmic goo till I get to the cheesecloth layer between sleep and not-sleep. I push and push—and my eyes pop open.

I land in my bed—damp, agitated, conscious—and roll over to find my husband breathing rhythmically. Looking at the slope of his shoulder moving up and down, I think, *Why didn't I think fast enough? Why didn't I just jump in the water and save my son?*

Days after the dream, I sit on a bench next to four other mommies. I watch my son pour sand from a dump truck into his pants. Shit, that means slinging him in the tub when we get home. Or I could let him run around naked until the sand on his ass dries and falls off onto the carpet.

"I simply can't get Sam to eat vegetables," a mommy next to me says.

"Cover them in cheese," another mommy says. "They'll eat anything covered in cheese."

I'm so bored I feel like crying.

A mommy looks at me and says, "What about you? How do you get Spence to eat his vegetables?"

What I want to say is, "I don't know about you ladies, but what I could go for is a big, hairy cock."

Instead I say, "I just do the reward thing. You know, if you eat four peas, you can have this can of Pringles."

The mommies look at me like I've suggested my son eat his own feces.

• • •

I don't have this mommy thing down.

I've been bringing Spence to this preschool for a couple of weeks now. Suddenly, all that we were together—our little club of two—is out in the open. My mommy shortcomings are on parade. I can't cook. I don't do crafts with dried pasta and glue on rainy days. Talking to other mommies makes me want to bite them.

Jesus. It took me two hours to make the twenty deviled eggs I promised to bring to the preschool Halloween party. The skin wouldn't separate from the white part, so I had to gouge each egg with my fingernail in order to peel it, leaving big dents. When I laid the egg-white ovals on the paper towel, each one looked like the surface of the moon. I sat in my kitchen and sobbed.

Spencer came up to me, covered from head to toe in red marker, looking like he had Ebola.

"Mommy's a little bit of sad," he said.

"Yes," I said, "I'm a little bit of sad."

A mommy at the school says, "I hide the vegetables in a tuna sandwich."

Cock, I think.

"All he tastes is the tuna fish."

Cocksucker.

"Or you can hide a piece of spinach between a cracker and a hunk of cheese."

Lick my juicy pussy.

"Peas are the easiest to get them to eat, because they're sweet."

Fuck me up the ass, Soldier. Then dick slap me till I cry for mercy.

• • •

Slow to Warm

A teacher comes out and yells, "Circle Time!!!!!"

The kids all run around like lab rats, screaming "Circle Time!!!!!"

Spence runs up to me and grabs my hand. "It's share time. What do I have to share?"

Just that your mom's a big loser, I think, because I forgot to bring a damn thing to share.

As we walk into the classroom I look at all the other kids bringing in shiny trucks, dolls with glossy hair, bags of marbles.

I bend down to Spence.

"What about your subway ticket?" I say, pointing to his pocket, where he keeps the tickets for the subway we ride to school every day.

"Yeah," he beams, reaching into his pocket. I know he is remembering our routine of riding the escalators, talking about the trains, paying for the tickets. I lean against the wall of the classroom, watching child after child show their loot and gab about it.

"It's a truck," says a boy with sandy hair.

"And where did you get it?" asks the teacher.

I can see where this conversation is going, and it's not far.

The other day, as I dropped him off, the teacher told me that Spence is "slow to warm." It sounded like she was saying he was unbaked bread.

Slow to warm, I thought. *That means . . . what?*

She continued, "So it will take him longer to become integrated."

Not wanting to lay my mommy ignorance bare, I nodded and said, "Yes, 'slow to warm,' I'll have to look into that."

At home I agonized over Spence being "slow to warm." Was it a physical thing, like his circulation was bad? Was it an intellectual thing, like he couldn't grasp simple concepts and had to warm up to them somehow by not approaching them head-on? Was it an emotional thing, like he carried things inside him—a human pressure cooker, ready to explode one day in violent preschooler rage? *What the fuck was "slow to warm"?!?!? Were we in serious trouble here?*

By the time I picked Spence up, I was close to tears. I pulled the teacher into a corner, shaking with shame and dread. She looked at me like I was a stalker, so I loosened my claw-like grip on her shoulder. I took in a long breath, and tried to steady my voice.

"What does 'slow to warm' mean?" I asked, preparing for the worst.

"Oh," she said, suddenly relaxing, "It means he's shy."

Relief flooded me and I felt like a doctor had told me that the black spot on my lung Xray, initially thought to be cancer, was just a mark from someone's coffee mug.

The sandy-haired boy sits down and the teacher calls on Spence to share. He reaches deeply into his pocket and fishes around, building the suspense, and pulls out a dog-eared ticket.

"It's a subway ticket," he says.

"Wow," says the teacher, looking confused.

"What's a subway?" asks a kid.

"It's underground," says Spence. "I go with Mommy."

After Circle Time, we all go outside to do an art project. Spence sits next to a girl who licks the edge of the table.

A mommy hands out pieces of construction paper cut to look like the facial features of a ghost: spooky, slanty eyes; button noses; smiley mouths. The kids begin to glue the pieces onto an outline of a Casper-shaped ghost. Spence glues down two eyes. He wants to make the nose another eye and begins to put an eye where the nose goes. A mommy reaches over and takes the eye out of his hand.

"That's not a nose," she says. "It's an eye. You can't have three eyes."

I could take her down right here. What a supreme idiot. Of course a ghost can have three eyes—It's a ghost! Christ on a stick.

But I just smile weakly at Spence, and remember to tell him, when we're on the subway, that it's fine for a ghost to have three eyes.

I revisit the dream. I lie in bed and conjure the pier, my naked son, and myself in layers of clothing. I see the moonlight. And I will myself there. I follow my son. He dives into the water—and this time, without hesitation or panic, I dive in after him. I feel the weight of the clothes pull me down, but my arms are strong, making sure arcs through the water. I go under. I see him suspended in bouncing, shifting light. I reach out, grab him, and swim toward the surface. The heavy clothing falls off of me and I kick easily back to the pier, my son safe in the crook of one arm.

I wake from the dream, my limbs light and floaty. Goddamn it, I finally got something right. I lift myself from the bed—maybe I'm still dreaming—and walk into my son's room where I see him under the covers, curled up safe. I scoot in next to him. I look at the ceiling and feel the roundness of his back against my arm. And I know, in one of those fleeting moments of clarity, that I can do this. I will learn how to do this. Because I cannot lose him.

When the Unthinkable Happens

Marie Myung-Ok Lee

HE LOOKED SO STILL. Jason, the boy who used the couch as a trampoline, suddenly motionless, as if dead, his tiny body sliding into the maw of the CT scan machine.

"It freaks most parents out, seeing their kid like this," the technician kindly told us.

He didn't know the half of it. Even at thirteen weeks, the speck on the ultrasound was constantly flipping, waving, swimming. As an infant, Jason wore out things with names like Exersaucer and Jolly Jumper. I could clip his fingernails only when he was sleeping. He willed his first step at nine months. Now, at eighteen months, he galloped everywhere.

Until he stopped.

The doctors were perplexed. Lyme disease? Lead poisoning? Stroke? Guillain-Barré? Muscular dystrophy? Brain tumor? Every day since our pediatrician had rushed us to the hospital, Jason seemed to lose a little more mobility. Every day, more tests, Xrays. A spinal puncture. They drew blood until the veins in his hands and arms collapsed; then they started sticking needles into his tiny feet.

Days later, still waiting. At a hospital barbecue, Jason, now paralyzed from the waist down, arrived in a little red wagon. The healthy siblings of other patients tore around the pavilion, gobbled hot dogs, clambered up a genuine antique fire truck. Jason, in his teddy-bear hospital gown and IV, stared sadly while I held his hand and tried to cheer him up. It seemed a million years ago when he would have been one of those little boys climbing immediately to the fire truck's high seat to pretend to drive.

What if he could never run and play again?

Our pediatrician began muttering that he was hoping for Guillain-Barré.

"Isn't that a terrible paralytic condition?" I asked.

He nodded. Then I wondered if he knew something we didn't. About the things that could go wrong, that weren't supposed to, when you hadn't even reached your second birthday.

It was time for the MRI. Sedated, a radioactive dye injected into his veins, Jason went in for a cranial scan, came out, woke up, fasted for a few hours, then was resedated, reinjected, and sent into the machine again.

After the last MRI study, the resident, who had a son Jason's age, came in to brief us—and burst into tears.

A very large tumor on his spinal cord.

Jason had weathered his hospital stay with equanimity, despite having to sleep tied down so he wouldn't pull out his IV lines and then, when he finally fell asleep, being woken for more tests. His only recreation occurred during visits to the toy room, where he had to play propped up in my lap. Before all this, he'd have wiggled off a lap after a few seconds. Through his fear, Jason tried to give me a smile, wan and brave. It made me miss all the more his crazy-wide smile—and even his crazy antics, like tumbling down a tube-slide headfirst. Being a very physical child, he was not very verbal. But even in his wordlessness, it was easy to see he just wanted to go home.

He needed emergency surgery to relieve the pressure on his spinal cord. He was moved into intensive care and started on high-dose steroids to tame the tumor's growth while the surgical team was being assembled. The ICU had no toy room, only an air of urgency: alarms blared constantly. A brain-dead child was taken off life support just after we moved in.

How could we explain to a preverbal toddler what was happening to him? Especially when we ourselves knew little, other than that a large tumor in an eighteen-month-old did not bode well. The oncologist began preparing us for a scenario that would include chemo and radiation, and, possibly, death. Soon after, a too-chipper man showed up identifying himself as a social worker "sent by the oncology department," bearing brochures for the local Ronald McDonald House.

It was going to be a long haul, in other words.

The nurses had warned us about 'roid rage. Jason thrashed, clawed at the needles taped into his skin. The only thing that calmed him was being pulled in the little red wagon. His father, grandfather, and I took shifts pulling him—for eight hours at a time.

At midnight, he finally fell asleep from sheer exhaustion. Jason had always had a frenetic, joyous personality, but at some point since his move to the ICU, he'd stopped smiling. Now as he lay sleeping, trembling from the steroids, I gazed at his little face, cheeks still bearing the chubby curves of babyhood, long beautiful eyelashes covering his Asian eyes. It all seemed so unreal, this windowless ward sealed off to visitors, the ghoulish chuff of the respirators constantly in the background. All I wanted was for this little boy to smile again. All I knew was that if anything happened to Jason, I would never be happy again.

Two months later, Jason underwent two major surgeries to remove the tumor that had insinuated itself onto his spinal cord and the surrounding bone. The recoveries were slow, the oncology wing just as urgent and forbidding as the ICU. The doctors had determined he had a rare kind of tumor that wasn't malignant, but it was on his spinal cord, and that was dangerous in itself. Also, there was still the possibility of it *turning* malignant. Complete, drastic removal was necessary—which meant sacrificing the tumor-damaged bone and then fusing what was left with the rest of his spine.

The little boy who'd endured so much awoke from his second surgery to find himself immobilized in a fiberglass-spica cast from his arms to his knees, with a breathing tube stuck down his throat and lines going into his hands, arms, feet, and neck.

His resilience amazed me. An error in removing the arterial line sent arcs of blood shooting across the room. The nurse had to press painfully on Jason's neck to quell the bleeding, but he bore it stoically. In fact, soon afterward, he began playing, using the top of his cast as a ramp for his Matchbox cars. Physical therapists who wanted to begin exercises to prevent muscle atrophy walked in to see Jason flapping his feet and his hands—the only parts he could move. They laughed and declared he was doing a fine job of exercising already.

My husband and I were grateful that Jason did not have a glioma or another type of tumor that might have killed him by age two. But putting an energetic toddler in a full-body cast and wheelchair was a different kind of torture. When he was well enough to go outside, I brought him to the playground, thinking he would enjoy the company of other children. But he began to yell, "No! No! No!" and so we left. I realized it was too painful for him to watch the other children do things he couldn't.

How do you explain this to such a young child? You can't. You can't even explain that the body cast is temporary, that he won't always be like this. Seven months' confinement seems like forever when you have only eighteen months to your name. He'd survived cancer, but what had he lost? After so many painful procedures during which I'd helped hold him down, I know he'd lost his trust in me.

When he woke from his first operation with the tube down his throat, little hands and feet restrained, he looked at me, tears streaming down his face, screaming silently, and I knew all he wanted in this world was for Mommy to remove the tube. And I couldn't. I left him that way for twenty-four hours until the nurses came in and with efficient, whip-like motions, tore the adhesive tape from those tender cheeks, then hauled out the unexpectedly long tube.

At his ophthalmologic exams, they forced his eyes open and

shined a bright light into them to check for tumors of the optic nerves; I held him down like a sumo wrestler. I held him down for Xrays. I held him down when they started the anesthesia for his surgery. I held him down when they inserted the anesthesia needles for his eighth, ninth, tenth MRIs to check for tumor re-growth.

Many months later, when he emerged from his cast like a wet butterfly from a cocoon, Jason taught himself to walk again—for the third time. Six months later he amazed everyone at the neuro-surgeon's office by walking in on his own.

His spine has healed, only a few degrees from straight. The possibility of tumor regrowth looms, but we have gone from three months to six months to a year between MRIs. My husband and I were relieved, only to find that at almost three, Jason is severely language delayed. In all our worry about his tumor and our joy at his being alive, we never noticed that he was not talking. Therapists use terms like "behind his peers" and "special ed." Having grown up with Korean cultural values that place education and achievement above all else—Jason's first present from my father was a Harvard rattle—I realize I need to put aside what I want Jason to be.

It's hardly surprising that he is suspicious of language. During his last MRI, when a combination of five nurses, doctors, and Mommy grabbed him to insert the needle and attach him to various monitors, he cried, "Let go"—even adding "please!"—to no avail. To the doctors who force on him needles and painful scans, he pleads, "No, no, mine!" as if to say, "It's *my* body, please respect it." But they never listen.

It is a dangerous cultural myth, aided and abetted by fuzzy

baby-products ads, that raising a child is all pastels and cuddles. Some weeping at an immunization, maybe an ear infection, is as bad as it gets—if you believe the Gerber commercials, or even the parenting magazines. This myth is so seductive, I suppose, because for most people, such a scenario is within the realm of possibility. But for Jason, for our friend's child who has Down's syndrome, for another friend's child with cerebral palsy, the map is completely foreign, and terrifying. What is normal behavior for a child who has constant seizures? Or for one, like Jason, who has suffered the trauma of surgeries on top of a missed year of playing and exploring—those crucial months between ages one and three?

When Jason was in the ICU or in his monstrous wheelchair, the sympathy and understanding poured forth. But now, with different problems, the slack is gone. He looks like any other toddler—but doesn't act like one. Unsure of using language, he tends to hit or explode into tantrums to express himself. Other toddlers walk quietly next to their parents. Set-free-from-the-cast Jason tugs, runs into traffic, thrashes, and breakdances on the ground when he doesn't want to go where I want him to (which is most of the time). Bystanders glare as if to say "Why can't you control your kid?"—and then I start feeling sorry for myself.

But I have to take a deep breath and think about what will be revealed later in the bath: the twice-opened Frankenstein scar over the length of his spine, the puncture where they collapsed his lung, the lateral incision splitting him almost in half, the ghostly scars of bedsores from his time in the cast. Soaping his back, my hand slips strangely over smoothness: he is missing those pearls-under-skin bumps, the pedicles, which have been destroyed by the tumor, as well as a rib, which was used to shore up the missing bone. His small body is a map of all he has borne.

Tonight he splashes, looks proud as Archimedes at all the water he's displaced. He runs away as I try to towel him off. When I try to get him to sleep, he won't stay in his bed. I've watched my friends with their children; they have calm nighttime rituals that involve reading books. Reading! As if.

But their kids are their kids. Jason is Jason. Later, I sneak back and see him sprawled on the bed, fast asleep, so peaceful that something in my throat catches. I think back to the day, over a year ago, when the oncologist came into our room to announce that Jason had a dangerous but not life-threatening tumor, and I can only thank God for his life, for the second chance given to a mischievous boy with a killer smile.

Our Drinking Problem

Katie Greenebaum

BY THE TIME MY OLDEST CHILD was one-and-a-half, she had lived in four apartments on two continents, one with no air-conditioning, one with no crib. She had suffered the onslaught of a baby brother, a jittery preemie who needed to be rocked for hours. Her strongest desire was for consistency and order, but all I could offer was constancy and chaos. Her reward for sticking with me was my total indulgence, which even then I saw as a mixed blessing. Early on, we struck an uneasy bargain. If I gave her everything she asked for, she wouldn't ask for much that was unreasonable.

I didn't need a how-to book to tell me I was headed for trouble. By the time she was two, she had a serious drinking problem and I was a textbook enabler. I had given her the first sip, after all. She was four months old, it was a sweltering New York summer, and we had just moved into an apartment with no cooled air. Abruptly, she stopped falling asleep on my breast. So we threw open the windows for the scant breeze, put her in bed, and listened to her scream. We became concerned about the neighbors—not their feelings, but their likelihood to call the authorities. My husband became convinced that she was dehydrated. So we reached for the amber liquid—half water/half juice—rested her favorite stuffed duck across her chest, and angled the bottle into her eager mouth.

Things deteriorated. Nora had no pacifier or security blanket, just her bottle to soothe nighttime fears. When she finished one she'd want another; she refused water unequivocally; she wanted to alternate juice and milk. Her legendary reasonableness flew out the open window. Her diapers weighed ten pounds in the morning. She'd wake up in the middle of the night with an upset tummy from the acidic commingling of juice and milk. After calming down, she'd ask for another drink. In the winter, if she had a cold, she'd often cough until she retched a horrible phlegm-based concoction halfway across the room.

I tried to wean her. But I wasn't brave enough to make a clean break. I simply asked her to be *slightly* reasonable: one bottle per night. Inevitably, after the first there was the demand for the second, and then there was my soft-shoe routine—cajole, beg, and plead— so unseemly for a thirty-something grown-up: kneeling on the floor, in nighttime rags, an agitated supplicant. And I could tell that Nora herself, even as she saw her request granted for the umpteenth time, didn't like being in charge. She'd be teary when I shuffled back into her room at 3:00 A.M., obviously delirious with exhaustion, with her spoils in my hand. She'd sniff in her tears and say, "But Mom, I just don't know how to go to sleep without a bottle." Then she'd look at me mournfully, as if she were holding this sentiment in to spare my feelings: *If only you were the type of mother who could teach me how. If only you could help me get through this stage with dignity.* As she took the beloved nipple into her mouth I could tell it was a pyrrhic victory for her. Once again she had shown that her mother couldn't be trusted to keep her word. I was weak-willed and hungry for approval. It was no wonder she still needed that sucking comfort: she was a two-year-old head of household—a terrible burden, even for a child as wise and knowing as my little girl.

How I wished we had managed to settle on a more benign "comfort object": a threadbare blanket, a one-eyed bear, even a thumb would have fewer calories and not promote tooth decay. All the modern parenting books seem to smile indulgently upon these habits, advising only that one wean slowly by restricting the places where habits can be indulged. But they all have ugly asterisks when it comes to bottle use, even with only water. Bottles with milk or juice at this age are so beyond the pale that they don't merit a mention. We were too far gone for advice.

Of course, Nora's bottle wasn't even a true transitional object. She never needed one outside the house. She was a model of maturity in the sandbox, a leader at the cut-and-paste station at school. There was something stoic in her even then, a preternatural awareness of life's struggles and indignities. But, by the time she was three, the bottle issue seemed simply to be one of sleep, and the fact that we had failed to teach her how to achieve it on her own. When I viewed the issue through this basic lens, I was able to see that what really bothered me was not the habit so much as the ugly dance that we had choreographed around it.

When it came to discipline, my parenting had a sort of *indulge, indulge, indulge, SNAP* rhythm to it that was confusing to my kids and exhausting to me. Whereas I had felt confident, even exuberant, in the face of having a baby—with my high threshold for disruption and my capacity to be distracted and amused—I was overmatched by the toddler years, which played to many of my weaknesses, most notably an overwhelming fear of conflict and a glaring lack of self-discipline and control. As for picking my battles, I preferred to wait most of them out.

What finally happened was this: a few months after Nora turned three, I claimed that all of the bottles were dirty and asked if she would mind having a sippy cup for just one night. Surprisingly, she complied. The next night I said the same thing and it worked again. A few weeks later, we were leaving for a friend's wedding, so I told her we didn't have room for both bottles and cups and since we used cups during the day, we would just bring those. Then, on the trip, I told her the hotel didn't allow juice or milk so she would have to have water in her now-beloved cup. At this point, I felt victorious, even though she was still sucking herself to sleep. By the time we got home she was ready to take a good look at just how old, scratched, and dirty her bottles had become and was able to say, "These are dis-gus-ting," and lightheartedly throw them away. After a few more months of sucking on cups, I made the surprising discovery that all the little rubbery inserts were mauled or lost. Couldn't she just sit up and drink a few sips out of a regular cup when she felt thirsty at night? Yes, she said, that would be fine. Four years after the drinking began, our struggles were finally over.

Of course, our struggles are never really ended. At eight, Nora is a judicious, mature, serious child who can't remember her bottle battles but finds other ways to test my parenting mettle. We still have our issues—candy, homework, television—and occasionally it seems as if she's still brazenly casting about for the egregious move that will suddenly transform me into the stern matron of her unconscious desires. She often pleads with me to be stricter with her younger brother and sister, or even with her, although she continues to refuse to comply when I try. Sometimes I worry that she's too attached to me, that somehow I failed to attend seriously enough to her, what with all of the new babies and new houses—that she holds herself in check all day at school like so many first children and then lies in her bed worried at night, staring at the ceiling, without even her bottle to comfort her. She will always be my first child, beneficiary of that initial rush of giddy love, but also the recipient of my first failures of authority. Still, time passes and things change. Some nights, just as I'm drifting off to sleep, I hear her little feet padding to the bathroom and my heart starts to palpitate just like it used to—*oh no, here she comes.* But she doesn't come. She wipes her own self, pulls up her own pajamas, arranges her own blankets, and puts her own self back to sleep. They do grow up, after all, despite the trick bottles we toss in their paths.

Eagle Moon

Elise Paschen

SNOWY FEATHERS TUFTED BY TAUPE. Out of reach it dangles, a flag attached by leather to a stick's peak. Alexandra is tapped on the shoulders with the feather and given her Osage name, *Heah Dawa* First Daughter.

Before her birth, my mother predicted our child would look Indian: olive skin, brown eyes and hair. When the nurse first handed our newborn to me I cried, grateful that she had arrived, that she was healthy, but then surprised by her rose complexion, having envisioned the baby my mother had described.

Alexandra, two years old, squirms in her father's arms under a canvas tent at the Grayhorse Dances in Oklahoma, while I am tapped and given my Osage name. The Tallchiefs, our family on my mother's side, are part of the Buffalo clan, and I receive the name *Tse-Hon-Ga-Wako* Sacred Buffalo Woman. Every year until my grandmother Tallchief's death, we would visit her in Fairfax. When I was my daughter's age, I would say, "Oklahoma, where the buffaloes roam."

Alexandra's sapphire-blue eyes shine and then widen as she is handed her eagle feather. As if it were a bird, she grazes it with her pointer finger. She has watched for this moment, as she waits for a new creature to approach. But then Alexandra grasps her trophy and the feather takes flight, swooping into the air, diving, until we take it from her hands for safekeeping.

In Rosemary's pickup truck, we bump over a cattle guard into fields thick with black-eyed Susan and Indian paintbrush. Across a pasture, a solitary black bull stares over the fence at his progeny. We climb out of the truck to feed the heifers.

Alexandra has no fear. But for me, since her birth, every day brims with danger. Whiteface Herefords, nostrils flaring, swagger across the field toward my daughter, who holds the pellet pail. Alexandra scoops the feed into her small hand and immense speckled tongues gobble and lap up the grain. Alexandra weighs thirty pounds and the heifers tower over her, one thousand pounds each. My daughter names the cows: "Come Daisy. Come Patches."

Our two-year-old squeals with delight, but Rosemary cautions, "Get back into the pickup. These cows could push against each other and crush us. They crushed our other pickup."

From her lofty perch atop her father's shoulders, Alexandra surveys the denizens of the field. She points to a small black calf nursing a brown heifer: "That's the mommy cow? That's the baby cow?" All creatures she observes are paired: mothers and babies.

When we return to Rosemary's ranch house, we explore the site of the winter Sweat Lodge. Alexandra discovers a baby flycatcher has fallen to the ground. I warn her—"Careful: don't touch the bird"—

thinking the mother might reject her young if handled by humans. But Alexandra loves animals and wants to hold it. She murmurs, "Poor baby." My husband and I exchange glances. She hovers over the bird while her father carefully perches the fledgling on bark and climbs a ladder to slip it back into its nest. He teeters—"Not much room in here"—as beaks open, expecting worms. I remember Alexandra, hours old, and how she resembled a baby bird, mouth gaping for milk, eyes closed, until she latched on to nurse.

But now she exclaims: "I hear the mama knock-knock-knocking." We all hear a woodpecker in a neighboring tree, drumming bark. Alexandra tugs on my sleeve and looks up at the tree: "The baby wants her mommy." She recalls her favorite book, *Are You My Mother?*, imagining the mother bird hunting worms while her fledging wanders off, mistaking a kitten, a dog, a cow for her mother.

Alexandra in her green and white gingham dress investigates the ground. She picks up sticks and uproots a dandelion, blowing all the fluff into the air. Her honey-colored hair tumbles around her face as she stoops down to observe an ant army carrying off a fallen fly. I lead her by the hand away from the war zone. Near the boulders of the Sweat Lodge she spies something and crawls on hands and knees over the stones. "Mommy. Look. An eagle feather."

As we drive back to the Black Gold Motel in Pawhuska, the moon begins to rise in the east. I think of a photograph in Alexandra's nursery taken after she was born, framed by a cow jumping over the moon. In the photograph she is so tiny and unknowable, her head covered with hair, her dark eyes wide open. According to the Osage calendar, this moon is called *Hiu'-wa-thi-xtha-dse Zhu-dsa bi* (the moon when the sensitive rose becomes red in bloom). I turn around to tell Alexandra about the moon, but her eyes are closed and she breathes deeply, clasped in the throne of her car seat. In her fist she clutches a scepter she will wear out and cherish: a snowy feather, at rest and shining, caught by a shaft of moon.

In Child Time

Alexandra Kennedy

IT'S 7:45 A.M. and I have thirty-five minutes to get my boys ready for the day. Jack, who's three, is heading to preschool, and Nick, who's two, is awaiting the baby-sitter. I don't so much walk through the house as ricochet. I snap up yesterday's papers and head down to the basement, dropping them in the recycling bin. I empty the dryer, start a load in the washer, grab the clothes basket, and shoot back up the steps. In the kitchen, by the dog dishes, I put the basket down, feed the dogs, pick up the basket, and march into the den. It's the modern parent's law of time management: never do one thing if you can do two. Three—recycling, laundry, dogs—and I am at peak performance.

In the den, the boys are on the couch under a quilt and fifteen stuffed animals.

"Come on, buddies," I say, rifling through clean laundry for matching socks. "Time to get dressed." Nick dives under the blanket, so I can only see a tangle of strawberry blond hair. (He insists to anyone who listens that his hair is "blueberry blond.") He will do his time, as he does each day, under the covers, ready to pop out and surprise his sitter, Chris. Three-year-old Jack looks at me urgently. He is our King Cuddles, a towheaded Linus with big blue eyes and a dingy, over-loved blanket. He would happily spend hours curled up like a puppy in our laps.

"I really want to be toasty under the blankets with you," he says.

"Sorry, sweetie," I say. "We don't have time. We'll be late for school."

In the thousandth of a second it takes for Jack's face to fall, I hear what he hears. "Sorry, I can't snuggle with you because we'll be late for school." For *pre*school! "Sorry, I can't snuggle with you because it won't leave enough time for me to write a grocery list for Dad."

The sight of a disappointed child—*my* child, disappointed in *me*—jams me up every time. As I fly through my morning, I can quickly factor into my list of priorities the boys' requests for a glass of milk, for finding a lost Buzz Lightyear, for breaking up squabbles, for unbunching socks. But a child who genuinely just needs me to stop moving and pay attention makes my brain short out. I may feel conflicted, but I am clearly reduced to one option. When I climb in between the boys, it's warm and smells like baby shampoo and Cheerios. I cross time zones, from a grown-up's to a child's, for the first of a dozen times that day.

For months now Nick has been making us laugh by shouting out "one more minute!" before every new twist in his day—before his nap, before going out in the car, before dinner. Of course he is throwing back at us our own harried grown-up language—the plea for "one more minute!"—but for Nick it is not sixty seconds. It is merely some promising piece of the future. In fact, my kids

In Child Time

understand exactly two things about time: it's morning when it gets light and it's nighttime when it gets dark. In between, they move in fits and starts from knight battles to guinea pig races to rock hunts to finger painting. Any one of those activities might occupy three hours or a minute-and-a-half.

Before Jack and Nick were born, I used to watch my friends with their children and wonder if I would ever have the patience for all that dawdling. As a parent, I now realize those kids weren't dawdling. They were just moving in child time.

That's a pace at which, left to our own devices, my husband, James, and I would never move. We are a well-matched pair, as they say of carriage horses. We take great pains to maintain some semblance of order in a house with two little boys, too many pets, my job, and his writing. We hand off and take on household chores and childcare almost wordlessly. We have surprisingly few arguments about who should do what and whether the division of labor is equal.

It is understood between us that we can only find peace in a house in which the plants aren't shriveled and the cupboard isn't bare. Sometimes our desire for order feels consuming, as if the one night we go to bed with dishes in the sink, the whole house will fall down around us as we sleep. The kids, of course, need structure to their day—and clean dishes—but they can't begin to comprehend the complexity of our household schedule, or why all the competing demands often keep James and me from being with them. As grown-ups we need to live in a civilized house despite the introduction of 212 little yellow bulldozers, sibling rivalry, and the constant restless motoring of little boys. The kids just want to have fun.

On a Sunday morning Jack announces to his father that he wants to do every jigsaw puzzle we own. Out of habit, James reduces this to a manageable project—maybe one big puzzle?—but then he takes it back. After a week of negotiating with the kids through an unflagging schedule of school time, baby-sitter time, meal time, tub time, nap time, bedtime, this is finally a decision he can make without looking at the clock. It is a relief to say yes. He pushes furniture out of the way to clear floor space, and begins to scour the closets for puzzles. He puts them together with Jack for hours, pointing to where pieces go only when Jack asks for help. By lunch, our home is carpeted with dinosaur dioramas, the planets of our galaxy, two farmyards, undersea panoramas, a herd of horses, a medieval village, and an antique store called "The Alphabet Shop," which carries items from A to Z.

On another day, an evening after work, I take the boys for a stroll along the river by our house. We poke sticks in a rotten tree stump for three minutes, four, five. When my mind wanders to phone calls and chores I need to do back at the house, I force myself to answer a question: Are those things more important than what I am doing right now? I tell the boys a story about the tree's long, good life and Jack spins it into a tale of giants and lightning bolts and a brave oak named Hank. As we finally walk home, the three of us swell with the satisfaction of having been finally, happily, in the present together, if only for a few sublime minutes.

After our walk, I find myself—as I do more and more—flashing ahead to a time when Jack and Nick will be young men, tall with deep voices, home just to visit. I can see them clearly as they sit around the dining room table, bringing back memories of childhood, teasing each other about their antics, remembering their favorite things. I know that what they will remember will be moments spent in child time. They will not, I trust, marvel that the house was always clean and that their parents were always on time. The boys will remember that age—before they knew how to read a clock—when time was plentiful, like air, and tomorrow was still defined as the day that will await you when you wake up.

Perhaps the boys will even remember my own favorite time of the day. Sometimes after dinner, if we are all tired and cranky from appointments and work and not enough time, James leaves the table of dirty dishes, steps into the living room, and puts on The Four Tops or Creedence Clearwater Revival or the Beach Boys—some relic from our own childhoods. Then we all go in and join him. We dance in circles, holding each other tight, shouting out the words. And when the song ends, and Jack says, "Again!" and Nick says, "One more minute!" James hits replay without a moment's pause and the four of us start all over again.

Pantless Superheroes and Chocolate Donuts

Sachin Waikar

"I HAVE TO CLOSE MY BUTT!" declares two-year-old Kayan as he stands naked in the half-full bathtub, his legs clenched together. It's an inauspicious start to our week alone. Kalpana, my wife, is at an out-of-town training program for her new job. My new job, at least for the time being, is to avoid a major bath mishap on my first evening as sole nighttime caregiver.

"What?" I ask, hoping I've misheard him.

"I have to close my butt so I don't have a poop in the tub!" The urgency in Kayan's voice mounts.

"Okay, bath's over," I say, scooping him out of the water while searching frantically for a towel. *You asked for this,* I remind myself.

We made several major decisions last year. I traded constant travel and long workdays (and nights) as a business consultant for the full-time-daddy track, hoping I could also devote some time to writing, my dream career, while my wife returned to her sales career. We also traded our small but stylish condo in the heart of Chicago for a house in a nearby suburb, where infrequent lawn mowing is considered an alternative lifestyle.

I expected to have difficulty finding local fathers in situations resembling mine. To ease the transition into my new world, I attended several kids' gym sessions with Kayan and Kalpana, and then alone with Kayan. As suspected, I was a male minority of one, except when dads on vacation or visiting grandfathers appeared. *Could they do this all day?* I wondered, observing their gleeful play with the tots. *Can I?*

I spoke pleasantly enough with the moms I met, bowing politely out of conversations that turned toward epidural timing strategies or high-intensity thermal hair-straightening. But I longed for the male camaraderie I'd enjoyed during early adulthood, before I'd become too busy with work to socialize much.

"I have no one to talk to," I lament to Kalpana when she calls at the end of her first day of training.

"What about Kayan?" she asks, half-seriously. I laugh, recalling the tub-talk. But her question stays with me. Granted, my son and I probably wouldn't have deep sociopolitical conversations, but how often did I have those with anyone? *It's not like you have any other choice,* I reason. *Maybe you'll even learn something from the little man,* adds the former psychologist in me (I'm a career collector). I decide it's worth a shot.

Our second afternoon alone finds me prone on the sofa trying to recover from my morning stint as a human jungle gym. I'm marveling at Kayan's energy when he tears into the room. "Swing me, Daddy! Swing me!" he urges, arms outstretched. I smile at my dimpled mini-doppelgänger and prepare a plea.

"Sorry, Kayan, Daddy's back is hurting." I hope the self-pity in my voice will discourage him.

"No, Daddy. You back not hurting. You back is stwong!" His black-brown eyes—a gift from his mother—shine with blind faith. I start to protest, but feel a warm current of energy run through me. And suddenly I feel stwonger. *The power of positive thinking,* observes the former psychologist as the dad swings his legs off the sofa.

Later, Kayan and I move—thankfully—into some pretend-play. "You be a lion, Daddy," he decides.

"Waaaaaaah!" I oblige, with a sound somewhere between a feral kitten's and a creaky door's.

"No, Daddy, that's too scary!" Kayan covers my mouth with his hand.

"Sorry, I'll stop."

A few moments pass.

Shyly, Kayan asks, "Daddy, can you be just a little tiny bit scary?"

After putting him to bed, I think about Kayan's request. A graph from my psychology graduate program comes to mind. It shows that anxiety and satisfaction share a curvilinear relationship—a fancy way of saying that a little bit of nervousness is optimal for us humans. Kayan was coaxing the pretend-lion toward the apex of that curve. Unfortunately, adults usually can't modulate stress levels with the same control a two-year-old has over his father's roars.

By the third day of our week alone I feel more confident in my stay-at-home shoes. Until I hear the scream.

Kayan is playing quietly in the family room while I work on a screenplay in the den. "AAAAAAAAHHHHHHHHH!" His shriek is right out of the zombie movie I've been writing. I freeze, then race to the family room. Visions of the undead, of ghastly puncture wounds, circle in my mind.

On my arrival, I find Kayan sitting calmly in the center of the room, an open book in front of him. *I'm too late. He's in shock.* "What's wrong? What happened?" I gasp.

"I was scweaming," he tells me, matter-of-factly. My concern melts into puzzlement.

"Yeah, I know, but why? Did you get hurt, or scared?"

"No," he replies, turning back to his book.

"Can you tell Daddy why you were screaming?" I'm unwilling to let this go.

"I'm a scweamer."

Again that night I contemplate my son's words. I imagine the types of statements we'd hear all the time if everyone were as honest as Kayan the Scweamer. "I must warn you that I'm a gold digger. If your net worth is not what it appears to be, I will seek a richer mate." Or, "I'm very excited about this promotion, particularly the golden parachute. My dedicated-employee masquerade paid off!"

The next day Kayan and I share our views on one of his new favorite shows. "I love *Superfriends!*" he announces, as we sit in front of the TV.

"Oh yeah? Why?" I probe.

Kayan considers this question for a moment. "Wonda Woman. She don' wear any pants."

"Yeah, that's why Daddy likes it, too." A true bonding moment.

That afternoon, we test the limits of our new candor at Kayan's gym class. "I love *Superfriends,*" he declares to one of the moms.

"What's he saying he loves?" she asks.

"The TV show with all the superheroes. You know, Superman, Batman . . ." I explain, searching for a quick way to change subjects.

"Oh. That's nice." She smiles at Kayan.

"Wonda Woman," he starts. *Uh oh.* "She not wear any clothes." If he knew how to wink, he'd do it right now. The mom's smile fades as she looks at me quizzically.

"Kids," I shrug.

The next morning is our last before my wife's return. While running some errands around town I treat Kayan to one of his favorite foods: a chocolate donut. Between dangerously large bites he exclaims, "I love cloch-et donuts!"

"Yeah?" I look at him in the rear-view mirror. "You know, Mama's coming home today. What do you love more—chocolate donuts or Mama?" I can't resist.

Without missing a beat, Kayan says, "I love cloch-et donuts AND Mama!" Couldn't have said it better myself. For a world of cloch-et donuts and mamas calls for a diplomatic strategy.

But there seems to be a cut-off age for effective employment of this technique. I'm definitely past it, as I find out when Kalpana returns. "I love you," I whisper as we hug, "and that new $35,000 Honda sports coupe."

Kalpana rolls her eyes and pushes past me to scoop Kayan up in her arms. "So how was your week together? Teach him anything new?" she asks.

"You asking me or him?" I reply, hugging both of them tightly. Behind her back, Kayan and I share a big smile. And I swear he winks.

Snapshot Daddy

Kerry Herlihy

THE TWO SNAPSHOTS ARE CRINKLED, both around the edges and through the middle. They are frozen moments my daughter peruses often these days. The first is of her leaning into her father, wearing his hat and African beaded necklace. They are both smiling into the camera. It is the first time in her two years that I can see his face in hers. The second is Daddy close-up, smiling serenely. It is from one of his two visits to Maine to see us.

Daddy and Mommy started as a one-night stand three years ago, progressed to intense passion, and ended up with a love that surprised both of us. When I got pregnant, Daddy was shocked and not entirely enthusiastic. I decided to move to Maine, near my family, to have S and take an extended maternity leave before returning to my life in Brooklyn. And here I am, two-and-a-half years later, still in Maine, daunted by the idea of motherhood in the big city. As for Daddy, he calls often and plays his peripheral role well. We slide along a continuum of like and love that unconventionally works for us.

The question surfaces as S comes around the end of the curly slide and lands on her feet.

"Where my daddy go?"

S looks at me using her new shrugging technique, shoulders up by her ears and hands that could hold a cocktail tray over her head. Shit. I thought I had at least another year to answer this guilt-inspiring question. Fresh out of clever things to say, I respond simply, "He's in New York."

"Oh."

And that is that. Until one minute later, when she asks again. And again. It becomes her mantra, except now, after three days, she can answer her own question.

"Where my daddy go?"

"You tell me, where is Daddy?"

"N'York."

"Right."

"Oh."

There is no longing, no pain, no early signs of all those inadequacies society expects her to have. Just a question needing an answer. Thinking I am ahead of the single-parent game, I give her the pictures to look at in addition to the "New York" answer that seems to solve everything. She insists on carrying them around the house, propping them up in the bathtub and putting them between her pillow and doll when she goes to sleep. I wonder if she clings to these pictures especially because her father's is a brown face, not unlike hers, give or take a few shades. Or maybe she does want her Daddy specifically. Or maybe she just likes the shirt he is wearing. I decide I need to remove my complex and muddled emotions from the picture party and see what unfolds.

Secretly, I am happy this Daddy kick is coinciding with our visit to see him in New York. These treks to the city are a fairly regular event when I feel like I need some urban renewal and S needs to see her Daddy. We pack up our old Ford Taurus with the never-ending road-trip necessities—raisins, Portacrib, Barney videos, and, of course, the Daddy photos—and head for the Bronx.

The ride is uneventful, a godsend in Mommy Land, and we arrive early at Daddy's house. He is not back from work and I sit there in the car waiting, feeling conspicuously white and from out of town. I try to conjure up that New York sheen I managed to pull off when I lived here. As I look around, I am struck by how easily S physically blends in here, as much as I stick out. She begins to kick and yell, "Out, Mommy! Out!"

We get out and take a walk around the block. S's shyness, which is a struggle at home, evaporates for the moment. She says hello to the men at the card table on the corner, to the girl walking home from school, to the scowling teenagers talking on their cell phones. Some respond, some don't. It's like she has acquired her take-on-the-world voice, which I find very New York. One man, who has soft curly black hair like hers, says, *"¿Nena, cómo estas?"* He looks at me and asks, "Does she speak Spanish?" I shake my head.

"She looks like she should," he responds quickly.

I agree.

At that moment, Daddy surfaces. He is all smiles. He reaches for S, but she turns away and peeks out from behind my leg. I want her to hug him and have the daughter-daddy moment I believed would be the logical extension of her questions, but no dice. She clings to me and sticks to her shy peekaboo game. I shrug it off and get Daddy to help us with the daunting task of getting all of our gear up six flights in one trip. We strap our bodies with bags and bundles and S carries the snapshots and a half-full box of raisins. I see her sneaking glances at Daddy in the elevator. I am really glad we are here.

Once inside with our things piled in the corner of the living room, I sink back into the center of the couch. S explores, being particularly drawn to the incense holder and the steaming radiator. I am tense with anticipation of her toddler ways. I am afraid she will ruin the reunion. Daddy tries to talk to her.

"Hey, muffin face, what you doin'?"

She looks at him, smiles, and runs into the other room. She races back ten seconds later and yells, "Mommy! Mommy!" as she dives for my lap. I pull her away and turn her to Daddy.

"S, honey, it's Daddy. Can't you say hi?"

"Nope."

She follows me to the bathroom, to the bedroom, to the kitchen. When I am talking to Daddy, she crawls on the chair next to me, puts her hands on my cheeks and turns my head so I only see her.

"Hi Mommy."

"Hi."

"What doin' Mommy?"

"Talking to Daddy."

"Oh."

"Can you talk to Daddy?"

"Nope."

As the days go by, S becomes more cantankerous. The coy smiles are now nasty whines and glares. The clinging has reached almost ridiculous proportions. She wakes up one night crying for Mommy. Daddy gets up and walks out of the room saying, "I know it's me. I know it. I'll go out here." S watches him go and outstretches her hands for me, immediately quieting as I pick her up.

The day before we leave, I manage to unglue S from my thigh by putting on Barney in the bedroom and slip away to the bathroom. Daddy is down the hall, trying his best to make the visit work. He is making bacon, S's favorite, and heating her milk on the stove because he has learned she won't drink it cold. I approach the bedroom door and I hear S talking. At first, I think she is singing with Barney, but I peek through the crack of the door to see her sitting on the bed with the Daddy snapshots.

"Hi Daddy. Muffin face? Nooo . . . Where my Daddy go? N'York . . . Hi Daddy. Hi Daddy. Hi Daddy . . ."

There's my sweet daughter's voice, the one I know back in Maine, talking to her Daddy for the first time since we arrived. I realize in that moment that snapshot Daddy is a lot easier to digest than real Daddy. Snapshot Daddy doesn't ask questions or talk to Mommy. He doesn't tell her to lie down and go to sleep or to leave the bathroom door alone. He just follows her around, smiles, and listens to her early-morning stories. In this moment, I think, S is using all her two-year-old coping skills to try to bridge the Daddy gap.

I walk in and ask, "Who are you talking to?"

"My Daddy. Mommy, where my Daddy go?"

"Your Daddy's in the kitchen. Do you want to see him?"

She pauses, looks at the snapshots, and says, "Okay."

And so we move down the hall, S running ahead, crinkling the photos with one hand and opening the door to the kitchen with the other. As she enters, I hear her say, in her take-on-the-world voice, "Hi Daddy."

The Fires of September

Rebecca Boucher

I USED TO THINK OF MYSELF, a mother of a toddler, as a sort of a twenty-four-hour E.M.T. I was supposed to watch Faith constantly to make sure she didn't choke or drown or take a header off the jungle gym. If I could read her a story in between close calls, all the better. Toddlers are, by their very nature, walking death threats to themselves. I always thought it was my job to be two steps ahead, covering everything in bubble wrap (be it real or figurative) to cushion the inevitable fall.

That concept was shattered on September 11, 2001. We lost many, many things. We lost neighbors and we lost our naïveté and we lost our sense of security. I, personally, lost my concept of mothering. I realized after that day that it is the purest delusion to think that you can protect your child from harm. You simply can't. All you can do is frame the harm, keep it in perspective, and hope it doesn't come too close. And if it knocks down the door like it did that day, all you can do is cope.

Faith was two-and-a-half years old when we saw the flames and the smoke of the World Trade Center attack from our Brooklyn home. She was with me while I was making beds, trying to keep our daily routine despite the horrifying view out the window and the constant sound of sirens. My husband, Tom, worked just one block away from the World Trade Center. He had called earlier, after seeing one of the planes fly by his window, to reassure me. "The worst thing to do is panic," he'd said. "Just go about your day. I'm going to be fine." Then I watched the first building come down. Until the phone rang again ten minutes later, I didn't think he had survived the collapse. When he called that second time, Tom spoke slowly. "Go get the kids at school," he said. "Pick them up and bring them home. I'm going to stay in the building until I can see where I'm going."

It was counterintuitive to put Faith in a stroller and go outside at that moment. The smoke was billowing over the river to us in Brooklyn. There was ash and paper everywhere. I wanted to shield her from the sight, the smells, the sounds of what was happening, even as I needed to understand it myself. As each successive fire engine roared by, sirens blaring, she would say, "Big fire. I'm scared." I started singing to her, songs I didn't even know I remembered. I sang "This Old Man," I sang old Carole King songs I had listened to in middle school, I sang anything that came into my head. Fighter jets were peeling out in the sky above us and she pointed to them: "Big noise." I kept singing.

Her siblings' school was in a tumult. The staff were trying to keep a visage of calm as they handed out dust masks to those of us who were leaving with our children. I was struggling to put one over Faith's mouth when the security guard took my arm. "You wear it," she said. I could only think of that video you see on the airplanes:

in the unlikely event that oxygen masks are needed, adults should adjust theirs before helping children. It makes sense, of course. If the mother is passed out, she can't take care of her kids. But it goes completely against the grain of every instinct. The ugliness of the situation requires that you ignore what you would like to do, and do, instead, what you must.

I gathered my three older children, who were scared, teary, and bewildered. I reassured them as best I could. I told them their father was fine, that he would be making his way across the Brooklyn Bridge on foot, and that it would take a long time. We went home a different route than usual because I didn't want them to see the Manhattan skyline, bleeding as it was. My ten-year-old son, Quin, looked up at the darkened sky and said, "Good, it's going to rain. That will put the fire out." I didn't have the heart to tell him he wasn't looking at a cloud; he was looking at airborne debris. I puzzled over how to reassure the older children while still maintaining Faith's sense of security. They had questions that deserved answers and she would, inevitably, be exposed to any information I shared with them. Faith had reached up to touch her brother as he walked alongside her stroller. Her hand holding his seemed to represent a contract of trust that couldn't help but be broken.

We were among the very, very lucky that day. Tom made it home hours later, covered in foul-smelling dust but alive. I got the children inside and then locked the door as if that, somehow, would protect them. I read to Faith from my childhood volume of *Winnie-the-Pooh*.

There was no way, ultimately, to shield her. She saw more than any two-year-old should see and, at the same time, saw less than many two-year-olds in other parts of the world have had to see.

The next day, I went outside to clean her playhouse. The ash was so thick I could make a path in it with my finger. It covered every aspect of her little world: her teacups and her tiny wicker chairs. You couldn't see through the windows. The toddler's world is defined, like it or not, by the vagaries of the world around her. No mother can change that. We can only sing to them while the fires are burning.

Inchworm Turns Three

Ericka Lutz

THE SAME DAY MY DAUGHTER, ANNIE, LEARNED TO WALK, she learned to run. For weeks, Bill and I had performed stoop labor, holding both upraised hands of our fourteen-month-old high-stepping daughter who collapsed into a sobbing puddle every time we let go. Our backs ached, our tiny, adamant child refused to detach herself or stop marching us around the house. Then one day, as Bill and I sat on the living room floor ten feet apart, Annie tod-dled alone between us. And again. Back and forth, from one hug to another. Proud, giggling, and . . . running.

At five, Annie announced, "I'm a girl who takes her time." At nine, Annie's baby teeth still refuse to loosen without surgical help. This is my daughter, Annie, the inchworm.

The inchworm, a small, hairless caterpillar, plants its front end, shifts its posterior prolegs toward its anterior prolegs thus raising its midsection high, higher, into a tall loop, then propels its front end forward in one swoop, an inch gained. So, too, my daughter, Annie, refuses change, stubbornly digging her metaphorical front end in until her midsection looms high over her head. Only when truly ready does she propel herself forward, in one gorgeous ground-gaining movement.

We are all born with tendencies and temperaments. But never were Annie's inchworm tendencies to resist and then embrace change so obvious as during the six-week period before she turned three, when my sweet girl looped high and pushed forward, and I was, all at once, the mother of a child, not a baby.

Six weeks before Inchworm turns three: Annie is finally learning to use the Big Girl potty. Bill and I discuss the concept for months before her skeptical hazel eyes; we present Big-Girl underpants and trips to the bathroom before putting on a clean diaper to go out in the stroller. She remains dubious.

Then one day: "We're going to Hudson Bay Café," I tell her.

"Do they have a bathroom there?" she asks.

"Yes," I say.

"I will go potty at the café." And that's that—we put on her underpants and they stay dry. For a few weeks, she asks to go to the bathroom in every business establishment we enter, for the fun of it.

"Do they have a bathroom in this store?"

"I don't know, honey. Let's ask."

Four weeks before Inchworm turns three: Annie moves to her own bed in her own room. She's had beds before—bassinet, crib, sidecar, crib mattress on the floor—but she's refused to fall asleep unless snuggled or in a moving car. Bill and I have lived with fatigue, parenting a strong-willed child who never slept more than two consecutive hours until she was two. For us, the family bed has been a necessity, not a lifestyle choice. Yet, Annie is turning three and I need to stretch out, so we get her a bed—a twin, a Big-Girl bed in her own room—where, one night, snuggled among forty-odd stuffed animals, she finally falls asleep alone.

Three weeks before Inchworm turns three: I wean Annie from the final bedtime nurse. She holds my nipple inside my shirt, she fumbles against me. "I want to nurse," she whispers.

"No, honey, we're already in bed."

"But I wanted to nurse before bedtime . . ." and she cries. It's been two days since she's nursed, each skipped session negotiated, or forgotten.

I hold her tucked against my body, warm and soft. A couple of shuddery breaths, and she stops.

"I'm so proud of you. You're my big girl. You're such a big girl, and I love you so much. You're doing such a good job with your weaning," I tell her.

"I'm weaned," she says.

I stop, myself unwilling to commit. But after all, that's what's happening. She's inched again.

"Yes," I say. "I think you are."

She stops, then: "But I am still Annie!" In the dark her face beams, smiling, proud.

I hold her close, her hand still on my nipple. "Yes, you are still Annie, you will always be Annie. Even when you are a grown-up. And I will always be your mommy and I will always love you very much."

"Some grown-ups are named Annie."

Inchworm Turns Three

"Some grown-ups are named Annie, but they are not you. You will always be you."

Her body relaxes. Her lower lip trembles.

"I'm very happy and proud but I'm also a little sad," I tell her. "It's a big thing, Annie, to be weaned. And I'm so proud of my girl. But it's okay to feel sad, too."

She is quiet, her breathing matches mine.

"Let's go to sleep now." It takes a few minutes for her to drop off to sleep in her Big-Girl bed, and I hold her close and watch her breathing settle.

The inchworm propels herself forward and then, after all the resistance and looping, she's in a different place. Too much at once; we're all shell-shocked. Annie reacts. She strains her foot and can't walk. She howls, preverbal again, rips toilet paper to shreds, and crawls across the floor. So much so fast, poor little Inchworm. Tomorrow she'll wake up with us in the family bed, put on her Big-Girl underpants, give me a hug, and move on.

In celebration of Inchworm's turning three, of Annie's massive accomplishments, we have a party. Actually, we have part*ies*. Plural. Four of them. One for extended family, one at home on the birthday day, one at daycare, and one for her little friends. Four parties? For a three-year-old?

Back in the day, I streaked my hair pink, wore basic black, and cultivated an attitude. I frequented Parisian cafés, read Marcel Proust in French, and never, ever expected I'd turn into a woman whose sleepless nights were caused not by nihilism but by worries over whether the balloon theme for my three-year-old's birthday party was noncommercial enough. To top it all off, I have the pre-birthday jitters. I brood: to bake or to bakery?

Party number one is for family and assorted adult friends. Annie's second cousin, Robin, has a birthday three days after Annie's so his mother and I combine forces to have a party at her house. I'll do the *pepperonata,* the beans and rice with all the trimmings, the tabbouleh, bagels, cream cheese, hard cheese, tomatoes, bread, and ice cream. Cousin Diane will do the chicken, green salad with figs and goat cheese, *caprese,* salsa, chips, and pick up the three cakes: chocolate, lemon, and other.
  "That should be enough," I say.
  "Oh, I've just begun!" says Diane.

Party number two lasts the entire day. It's her birthday. Bill and I wake Annie with presents in the living room, and she has just finished carefully opening these (she's gotten faster since party number one) when there is a knock on the back door—Grandma and Grandpa. They've spent the last four hours constructing a modular play structure in the backyard. Annie requests a fancy birthday lunch—chicken without the skin and boiled carrots. Grandma stays for chocolate cake.

Party number three is at Annie's daycare and I attend, wracked with guilt at not having invited any of these lovely kids to Annie's at-home children's party. But the daycare's nonexclusionary policy states that if you invite one child you have to invite them all, and six more kids and twelve more parents is more than I could cope with. The children have baked muffins and the teacher places three candles in Annie's.

"Blow, Annie."

"Make a wish and blow, Annie."

Annie stares so long at the burning candles that the other kids get antsy. Then she blows them out easily. She's become a pro.

The kids' party, the fourth and final one, almost does me in. My morning is calamitous. The bagel shop is out of bagels, which necessitates an emergency change of menu. The ice chest is discovered to be lined with black mildew. The seven-minute "no-fail" frosting requires forty-five minutes of continuous beating and then overflows, generating two kitchen fires. Annie sleeps through it all on her back, full-froggy in the family bed, tiny snores issuing from her lightly freckled nose. We make it to the park by ten-thirty, just as the guests arrive.

Then it's over. Two sets of parents aren't talking to me because I put candy on the cake. The kitchen is covered top to bottom with green and blue frosting, and Bill and I numbly wade through LEGO and puzzle pieces, shove aside piles of torn wrapping paper, and collapse on the rug.

Annie comes and sits on me, freckles sprinkling her nose, big brown hair messy, smile wide. Definitively three and still Annie, the Annie she will always be.

"It is my birthday," she tells us.

"Next year, Paris," I announce. After all this hoopla I need to regain my youth. I just know we have an intense year of changes ahead of us; Annie resisting, looping forward, and reacting. And I can picture my little inchworm in a matching black turtleneck and beret, blowing out four candles lodged in her chocolate mousse.

Field Notes from the Playroom Floor

David Carkeet

THE SONOGRAM WAS MURKY, but there could be no mistake: my wife was carrying twins. While she seized my hand and tried to come to terms with this kink in nature, I stared at the screen with a single thought: *Research Opportunity!* Many linguists had studied their own singletons, but none had studied their own twins. I could be the first. I would have to work fast, though, to prepare myself for the data that would soon fill the house. My linguistic specialty was Old English as spoken around 1000 A.D., and its speakers weren't exactly squirming with life.

I read Roger Brown's *A First Language*. I read Lois Bloom's *Language Development*. I read Ronald Scollon's *Conversations with a One-Year-Old*. I sent off to the NEH, NIH, and NSF for grant applications. I foresaw funding and acclaim for something I would be doing anyway—hanging out with the kids.

But in Anne and Laurie's first year, I learned that I could not be both father and observer. I would like to say that I threw my notebook aside and declared, "By God, I'm going to enjoy these babies." The truth is I spaced out. My analytical self took a holiday. I understand now what happened. Child care requires a mental fleeing of the scene on a regular basis. I've seen it in family-center playgroups, in preschools, and behind the bars at the zoo. Watch how a mother chimp's eyes glaze over. She knows she's in it for the long haul.

So I moved on to other interests, other projects. But I continued to track the girls' linguistic progress. I observed that their first words were identical—"ball" and then "bye bye"—and that a gesture obligatorily accompanied each. They would not say "ball" without clutching a ball and thrusting it forward in their hands, and their "bye bye" always came with a squeezed wave. I noticed that at the end of a large family picnic, as the farewells were flying, fourteen-month-old Laurie worked her hand feverishly at her side, privately squeezing with every "bye bye" she heard, even though most of them had nothing to do with her.

As for the first two-word sentence, always a major milestone, my notes tell the story for Anne, then twenty months old: "Anne last night produced 1st 2-wd. sentence. She was putting on wool hat, taking it off, etc. I was lying on floor looking up at her, she looked down, eyes suddenly glimmering, & said, *dada ah* ('Daddy's hat'), whereupon she instantly tried to put the hat on me. Very exciting." And very odd, I now think, that I could seriously write "whereupon" in these notes.

The single most important principle I learned from my observation is that children will do their own thing on their own schedule, and when they go astray they will gleefully defy an adult's efforts to correct them. Probably the most dramatic example of children's linguistic independence is their ability to create words that have no connection with the adult language. I don't mean babbling. I mean *words*, consistent sounds with consistent meaning. Just after she turned two, Anne took to saying "buck-a-buck." She said it a lot. During a walk in the neighborhood, I remember a menacing seven-year-old boy laughing at her and saying to his friends, "This kid says 'buck-a-buck.'" (When you're with two-year-olds all day, seven-year-olds suddenly seem large and threatening.) But Anne wasn't just making laughable noises. She was communicating. She uttered "buck-a-buck" only when she encountered an unfamiliar object, and she would invariably point at it as she spoke. "Buck-a-buck" clearly meant "what's this?" There is little similarity in sound between "buck-a-buck" and "what's this?," so the expression was a spontaneous coinage by her.

Other linguists have observed this kind of thing. In *Learning How to Mean*, British linguist M.A.K. Halliday reports many examples from his son, Nigel, at a strikingly early age. At nine months, Nigel said "na" with the consistent meaning of "give me that." When Nigel said "mnng," it meant "do that right now." His "uhnnn" meant "it's nice to see you—at last!" I like the nuance of that "at last." I like it when a stay-at-home linguist makes a claim with reckless confidence.

Sadly, these coinages die out within a few months of their appearance, supplanted by adult words—though not always directly. Instead of going right from "buck-a-buck" to "what's this?," Anne went through a stage when she would point, pause, and say "this is?" The eerie, predictable way she said this about one item after another gave the impression that she was on a mission to catalogue the world. Now it reminds me of the interview style of Charlie Rose: "And you felt this way because?"

Children's independence extends into grammar as well as vocabulary. Like many toddlers, Anne and Laurie learned the object form of pronouns first ("him") and used it for all purposes. They said "him go" long before they said "he goes." If I said, "That's his car," they agreed with a firm, "That him car." Their reanalysis of adult data was so aggressive that in their pronunciation of the word "history" they operated on the "his" that they somehow discovered within it and produced "himstory." "History" isn't ordinarily part of the toddler lexicon, and I wasn't reading Winston Churchill to them. It was Christmastime, and they were singing of Rudolph's future fame: "You'll go down in himstory."

When the girls sang those words, all I could do was stare at them in wonder. I certainly didn't correct them. They were like young scientists momentarily working with the wrong hypothesis, and eventually they would find the right one. Besides, correction would have had no effect. For years, both girls said "upside over" for "upside down," even when I repeatedly prompted them with an exact model. "Say 'upside down,' girls." *"Upside over!"*

One particularly noteworthy incident occurred during a visit with the girls' Aunt Connie in New York. A gaunt, chain-smoking, retired career army nurse, Aunt Connie had no children of her own and therefore was a child-rearing expert. When Anne and Laurie showed up for a first-time visit, at around age four, Aunt Connie was not pleased with the way they pronounced "s." Their rule for making a word like "cups" was "cup" + floppy wet lip noises; "desks" was a deluge. Connie sat them down on the couch and lectured them, making them say "s" over and over. "Say it," she said, pointing a bony finger at them. "Say 's.' Say 's'." The girls, earnest pupils, dutifully filled the air with their spray.

What were the fruits of this instruction? Certainly not any change in their pronunciation. But there was an effect, of sorts. I cavesdropped on the girls later during the visit, when they were alone, acting out some drama with their dolls. It became clear to me that they had given one of the dolls—the villain—a new name. They called her "The 'S' Lady."

I might have let my Research Opportunity slip by, but I was astonished again and again by the data that came my way when I wasn't even looking for it.

Bedtime for Milo

Ayun Halliday

I'VE NOTICED A TREND IN TODDLER LIT. No matter how jacked up the main character is for most of the book, he will fall asleep on the final page. It doesn't matter if he's a fire truck. Flip to that last page and you'll find him snuggled under a patchwork quilt, angelic and presumably down for the night. I guess little ones hearing these adventures in their jammies are supposed to take the hint.

My two-year-old son, Milo, doesn't have a regular bedtime ritual. Sometimes when we're out late visiting friends, he conks out on the subway back to Brooklyn, not even waking when he's yanked from his snowsuit. Other times, he's so worn out from a napless afternoon that he loses consciousness at the dinner table, chewing stoically even as his eyes roll back in his head. There are nights when I am the one who can't keep my eyes open, leaving Milo and his older sister, Inky, to race around our small apartment in tutus and their father's shoes. Inky enjoys the traditional bedtime story when it's offered, but Milo has yet to meet a board book that can compete with my breasts. Getting Milo to sleep is no big deal, not while he's still nursing. Apparently, my milk is a miracle elixir from the land of Nod, and the dairy operates twenty-four hours a day.

Overpowered by the twin fleshy engines he recently dubbed the "nursing guys," Milo drops off without a fight, but a few hours later, he's up, ready for another round. He sleeps, as did his sister for the first three years of her life, between me and his father. When Inky was born, I worried that my sleeping body might accidentally smother her in bed, but I quickly learned that mothers are hard-wired to awaken at even the most muffled peep from their young. Fathers don't seem to come equipped with this internal alarm system. At 1:00 A.M., when Milo starts shrieking like a surprise fire drill, Greg rolls onto his side and snores louder. His eyes screwed shut, Milo's panicked bleating continues until I seize him by his ankles and drag him into position alongside me. Sensing the nearby presence of warm milk, he turns his head, latching on mid-squawk. Immediately, his eyebrows lift, his limbs stop flailing, and he snuffles a high-pitched sigh of profound relief.

I, however, feel my face calcifying into a mask of irritation, even as I tell myself to remain as close to the dream state as possible. I bury my nose in the dandelion tuft of Milo's never-been-cut yellow hair, which has a sedative effect on those rare occasions when he's been put to bed freshly shampooed. But even if his hair smells terrific, the awkwardness of this side-lying, breast-chomping, head-sniffing pose becomes painful after thirty seconds. I rearrange our bodies and wait for him to slip back into sleep. If my book is out of reach, I pass the time by staring daggers into Greg's undisturbed back. I am vexed by a 1930s-style film that flickers through my head, in which a harried

father in a white nightshirt sterilizes bottles and paces with a cater-
wauling lace-bonneted infant while Mother slumbers on in her neg-
ligee. Here I am, a modern woman, imprisoned by the frequent
nocturnal urges of a two-year-old whose breast fixation outstrips
anything displayed by that paternal lump on the far side of the mattress, even in the earliest days of our romance.

"Milo, nighttime is for sleeping," I whisper when he appears to
be almost entirely out. If subconscious suggestion can wean smokers
from cigarettes, perhaps it'll be of some help to me. "If you open
your eyes and the window's dark, that means it's sleepy time and you
should just cloooooose your eyes and go right back to sleep. Sister
sleeps and Daddy sleeps and Mommy sleeps and Milo sleeps." Illu-
minated by the street lamp's light filtering through the blinds, he
looks as blankly receptive as someone undergoing hypnosis. Good.
I ease my nipple out of his mouth, taking caution not to accidentally jostle him, which in the past has resulted in an unforgettable
snapping together of his jaws.

His face crumples. "Other side," he wails. Damn. "Nurse!
NURSE!" If this were *ER* and he were a handsome young attending,
I'd slap him for ordering me around in such a presumptuous, rude
tone. As his lactating mother, I have no choice but to wrap my arms
around him and roll us both 180 degrees, granting him access to my
right breast from a spot perilously close to the edge of the mattress.
I buttress him with a small buckwheat pillow the way I did when he
was a puny newborn, unable even to roll. I never quite believe he'll
fall out of bed until I awaken to the *thwok* of his precious little body
hitting the hardwood floor. This time, he falls asleep shortly after his

demands are met and stays that way. I pull him away from the edge and still he sleeps.

Unfortunately, I am wide awake. I listen to the music blaring from passing cars and couples sounding like they're going to murder each other on the way home from the bars. Unable to stand the yammering of my alert but unoccupied mind, I switch on the light. Look at the little criminal, sprawling in his chaste green-and-white-striped union suit. He's had it for three Christmases in a row and is only now starting to outgrow it. He's in that newborn Aztec warrior pose, his arms bent and bracketing his head. In the carelessness of sleep, he looks like an unworn, stubble-free miniature of his father. I allow myself to feel a little more charitably toward them both, telling myself that in some ways, it's a gift, Milo's chronic destruction of my chances for a good night's sleep. Books are my passion and as the mother of a two-year-old and a five-year-old, when else am I going to find the time to read? I can usually clock a hundred pages before he's up again, howling for more.

The scene is replayed at two and, if Milo has refused to eat any thing at dinner, again at four. He never seems to come fully awake, thank God. We once stayed overnight in the home of acquaintances whose two-year-old observed a graveyard shift that involved requesting at least three different kinds of beverages before he successfully screamed himself downstairs, where he was plopped in front of a favorite feature-length video, which he watched to completion. Occasionally Milo will interrupt one of his post-midnight snacks to utter one of his signature phrases—*No want wear pants* or *I see a movie tonight*—but these seem to be little more than routine

Ayun Halliday

system maintenance, a sort of synaptic checklist to verify that everything's functioning according to code.

The worst affront to the tattered remains of my beauty rest is the last, which hauls me up from an unexpectedly deep, drooling sleep. It's growing light outside the blinds. Where am I? Oh yes, Inky's room. She'd cried out from a nightmare shortly after Milo's last feed and I'd stumbled in here like a much abused indentured servant, the one the masters are working into an early grave. Must have dropped off. I pause to gaze at my beautiful daughter, who remarkably is not roused by her brother's banshee shrieks. At his age, she pretty much slept through the night, even though she also nursed and shared our bed. Oh my God, what if we've missed some deadline with him? I try to imagine a long-bodied thrashing grade-schooler kicking me awake at regular intervals, eager to avail himself of a pleasure his advanced age would prevent me from permitting him in public. Sometimes I overhear mothers of nine-month-olds describing how much easier their lives are now that their babies are out of that crazy nurse-round-the-clock newborn phase. "I feel sane again now that he's *finally* sleeping through the night," they laugh, cuddling their toothless, hairless crawlers as I experience the dismay of someone tied to train tracks. This is my lot. I drag myself out of Inky's bed. "Coming, Milo. Mommy's coming. Mommy's here."

122

I Not Spill

Jennifer Margulis

MY DAUGHTERS AND I are dining at the café of our local food co-op. Somehow I was able to navigate two bowls of soup, two toddlers, a large salad, and some shish kebab to a table without spilling anything or dropping Athena, who insisted on being carried. Now Athena, not yet two and not quite two feet tall, is standing on her chair throwing cucumbers and spinach leaves on the ground. Hesperus, three, is begging me for Goldfish. "Why does she have Goldfish, Mommy?" she asks of an older girl who is sitting at the next table by herself, eating quietly while her mother finishes shopping. I rush back and forth to gather silverware, extra napkins, water, and the twelve other things the girls need right away. Toddlers, pregnant women, and hypoglycemics all have this in common: when they need to eat they need to do so urgently. But today my daughters are more interested in the details than the dinner. Instead of eating peas, Athena puts them in her mouth, bites them, whines loudly, and then spits the saliva-moistened bits into my hand. I am a human trash can, a nose wipe, a comfort blanket. Spitting out food is one of Athena's favorite tricks.

Hesperus, in the meantime, has found other prey than the lamb on the shish kebab. She wanders over to the older girl and barrages her with questions.

"I'm three," she says, holding up three fingers and counting them off instructively as she does so—"One, two, three! See? Three! How old are you?"

"Ten," answers the girl.

"Ten?" My daughter is indignant. "Why are you ten?" Hesperus turns back and scowls at me. "Mommy," she accuses, "that girl said she was ten. Why is she ten and I'm only three? I want to be ten too. And why does she get to eat Goldfish? I want Goldfish too! Mommy, can I have Goldfish?"

Hesperus often wears us down by repetition. She asks the same question (Can I go outside now? Can I watch a video? Can I have a piece of candy, just one piece, please?) so many times that, just to stop hearing it over and over again, we give into part of her request (Yes, after you get on your coat and boots; Just one episode; No candy right now but if you take a really long nap and rest really quietly you may have a piece when you wake up).

I eat the roasted lamb with one hand and feed Athena spoonfuls of soup with the other—she's so mastered the use of cutlery that she's back in the baby stage, refusing to hold the spoon herself and wanting me to feed her. Getting little response from the ten-year-old, Hesperus returns to our table and starts picking the raw mushrooms out of the salad and eating them. "I love mushrooms!" she cries. Last week it was bamboo shoots. She ate every bamboo shoot out of the order of Chinese food my mother brought over and before each mouthful she squealed, "I LOVE BAMBOO SHOOTS!" except sometimes she forgot what they were called and said, "I LOVE BOO BOOS!" or "I LOVE THESE THINGS THAT I AM EATING!" The list of Hesperus's favorite foods includes comestibles I never knew existed until after I graduated from college: whole wheat fusilli, kale, escargot, mangoes, pomegranates, papaya, and brewer's yeast. She even claimed to like a salty Chinese candy we bought in Hawaii, one of the most unpalatable things I have ever tasted. Hesperus will try anything, eat anything, and takes it as a point of honor to like unusual foods.

Athena, on the other hand, has never been interested in eating. She threw up absolutely every new food we introduced her to as a baby and nursed almost exclusively until she was well past a year. She still nurses often and eats almost nothing. Nonetheless, she has grown plump and healthy—maybe on the bath water she drinks by the cupful every time we bathe her, or on the bits of food that reach her digestive system before she spits out the rest in my hand.

Although she insists that I feed her every mouthful, Athena is eager to drink her water from the grown-up-girl cup on the table by herself. "If you want to drink you need to sit on your *tuchas,*" I say. Athena instantly sits down and turns her attention to the task of drinking. She takes this very seriously, holding the cup in her two pudgy hands and looking into its depths, as if she can read her future there. "Mommy, I not spill," she assures me, interrupting her reverie and staring at me out of gray-blue eyes. Her gaze unfailing, she shakes her head as she promises again not to spill the water, straight red-brown hair flying around her pale face, and then turns her attention back to drinking. She brings the cup to her lips, tilts it slowly, and sips a droplet of water. She places the cup back down so carefully that its contact with the table makes no noise.

"Mommy, I not spill!" she triumphs, looking at me again but smiling this time. Athena's smiles, though not rare, are often unexpected. They fill out her face in a way that lets me imagine her grown-up—a serious young woman, a Jewish-Irish-Italian beauty. Confidence boosted, Athena drinks again. This time, however, she is not as careful. She brings the cup up abruptly, throws her head back in time to take an enormous gulp of water, and drenches her face, neck, shoulders, and shirt with the rest of the water.

"Shit!" I furiously snatch the cup from her.

"Ut oh," Athena looks at me sadly. "I spill. I all wet."

"Damn it, Athena."

Hesperus stops staring longingly at the ten-year-old girl and watches me intently, gauging how angry I am. The look of hurt on Athena's small face makes me instantly sorry. I drain our water-logged food and wonder why I am not more like those *other* parents who never yell at their children for spilling things and always bring a change of clothes with them, in a waterproof bag, even to the grocery store.

We finish the damp lamb and I offer a wooden skewer to each girl. Athena brightens as she realizes she can use the skewer to fish for tofu in the salad. She needs to kneel for this activity and she bends her whole body and all of her concentration to capturing the tofu. Her aim is inaccurate, her gray eyes keen, her face so serious it looks almost suspicious under line-straight coppery bangs. She manages to spear a piece and wobble it up to her mouth. The spilled water and soaked shirt forgotten, a look of satisfaction lights up her face as she eats her catch.

"Hey," Hesperus says, "I want to do that too!"

The two girls use their spears to impale tofu, pinto beans, and tomatoes from the salad. I watch them smiling, remind myself to buy toothpicks to make little hors d'oeuvres like my father did when we were little, and think about the time Hesperus woke up in the middle of the night and claimed she could not sleep because she was hungry. I brought her a bagel and cream cheese and sat on the edge of her bed while she ate. First she licked the cream cheese entirely off both halves of the bagel, as systematic and purposeful as a mother cat licking a kitten clean. I stifled my irritation—it was late, I was tired, I wanted her to finish her snack and go back to sleep— and forced myself not to comment. After all the cream cheese was gone she bit into the bagel, munching it with such enjoyment that I could not stay grumpy. She finished every crumb and, her tummy full, slept later than usual the next day.

"Let Athena do it her own funny way," Hesperus sometimes tells us when Athena protests as we try to help her put one foot in each pant leg instead of both feet in one leg or turn an upside-down book she is reading right side up. I follow my three-year-old's advice, ignore that they are both waving meat-impaling punge sticks in the air and that neither has the manual control to keep the sticks in check, and let them enjoy the satisfaction of spear-fishing the salad.

Floating Cups, Quicksand, and Sudden Death

Catherine Newman

Uncle Keith is visiting us for the holidays and Ben, newly three, is hopping around Keith's chair on one foot, eating a clementine and pummeling him with a million questions: Do you like green olives? Do you *not* like melon? Is my daddy your sister? "Who are your grandparents?" he asks at some point, and Keith patiently catalogues them. They're all dead. "Last, there was my mom's dad," Keith concludes, "Grandpa Ray." Ben has deciphered the pattern of this conversation. "Is *she* dead too?" he asks. Poor, hapless Keith. It was, we are quick to reassure him later, quite natural to assume that "she" would *not* mean Grandpa Ray—on account of it being a female pronoun and all. But Grandpa Ray is, indeed, who Ben means to be asking about. "Yes," Keith nods solemnly, "she is. My mom died a few years ago."

Ben's face becomes a still-life of terror. It's as if a door has cracked open from the sunny, flower-filled meadow where his brain has been living onto a howling hurricane, teeming with demons, just outside. *Mothers die.* His eyes turn into black saucers and he stands perfectly still. The fear is so huge and palpable—it's like another person hulking in the room with us. I kneel down by him. "Is that hard to think about?" I ask, but Ben doesn't want to talk.

So now we've graduated to a new level of worry—and we'd barely grown accustomed to even the most mundane of Ben's fears. Of course it's entirely normal for toddlers to be fearful, but it's just so sad. One day you have this joyful child bouncing through your house like a piece of Silly Putty, and the next day he staggers to the breakfast table all haggard with worry, like a promising extra on the set of *A Clockwork Orange*. You can practically see the fears lounging around in his psyche, helping themselves to another bowl of cereal while they plan their latest attack: "Okay, you—yes you, Unshakable Terror of the Blender—you're up today." We miss the relatively relaxing days of Ben's simple *aversions*—pubic hair, hard-boiled egg yolks, jazz—however passionately expressed. Now the world is suddenly populated by malevolent forces—lions, reptiles, the *beep-beep-beep* of a truck backing up—that are too, as Ben puts it, "afrightening" for words.

"It's not actually the height itself," my father once said about his acrophobia, "it's the *falling and dying* I'm afraid of." And when Ben developed his sudden phobia around drains, it was with similar precision: it wasn't the drains proper that frightened him, it was the *getting sucked in*. His father, Michael, and I got backed into endless debates about what could and couldn't fit down the drain.

"Can a speck of dust go down it?"

"Yes."

"Can a leaf?"

"Maybe a tiny one."

"Can a peacock?"

"No."

"Can an ant?"

"Yes."

Eventually he'd try to trick us. "Can a boy?"

"No, sweetie. A boy could never go down the drain."

"What about a *tiny* one, tiny as a tiny leaf?"

At one point, Ben didn't bathe for two entire months, and we sponged off his sticky toddler self as best we could. He even refused the cool blue of a swimming pool. "What's *that?*" he asked, and pointed to the gurgling gutter running underneath the pool's ledge. Poor guy—kicking his little legs anxiously in a ballooning blue swim diaper, and I tried to pull a fast one. "Uh, that's a, um, *water shelf*, honey," I said vaguely. "You mean, like a drain?" He turned his honest brown eyes to my face. "Um, yes, kind of like a drain." Scared kids are not stupid.

So, nobody wants to get sucked down the drain. Fair enough. And Ben has always been petrified of snakes in that kind of primal, shuddering way that seems totally logical to me. We've been reading *Babar the King,* and there's this part where the Old Lady frightens a brown snake who responds by biting her. Her arm swells up and she has to go to the hospital but then she's better by the morning. Ben is completely preoccupied by this scenario. (Admittedly, the *Babar* books are a little creepy, even beyond their weird colonial apologies. One of *my* strongest early childhood memories is of a different *Babar* book, where the old king eats a poisonous mushroom, turns a vivid, wrinkly green, and dies. Fear-wise, this scene was right up there with quicksand. And with the fiery Injun Joe cave scene in *Tom Sawyer*—four birthdays in a row, I blew out the candles on my cake and wished, quite simply, that I hadn't seen that movie.) Now we spend a lot of time playing "snake bite." Ben says, "Oh! I'm a brown snake and I'm afrightened!" and then he bites your arm and pretends to rush you to the hospital, where your arm swells up, but, luckily, you are likely to make a full recovery by morning.

So, nobody wants to have a swollen arm—even if it's just overnight. Snakes are out. But in truth, Ben has often been overtaken by fears that are wholly unfathomable to us. Like the *fear of things floating in the bath*. It's been kind of a Catch-22: we seduced him back to the bath with a flotilla of plastic toys, but then they end up floating in the water, which scares the bejesus out of him. "Mama," he cries, "that cup's floating! Grab it! I'm getting out of the bath! I'm getting out! Help! Dry me off!"

Conversely, there are things you'd think Ben might be afraid of, but which seem not to scare him at all. Once, when we were visiting my parents, their carpenter friend, Brian, came over to look at their roof. Brian only has one leg, and we were all standing around outside talking, and when Ben came out to join us, I thought, *Uh oh*. Ben walked this big circle all the way around Brian, peeking underneath him surreptitiously, before coming back over to me. "What's happening to Brian?" he whispered. So I said, "If you have a question for him, why don't you ask Brian yourself?" Ben walked over to him, waited politely for a break in the conversation, then asked, "Um, excuse me Brian, but can you please tell me—where is your other shoe?" Utterly fearless.

Which is more than I can ever say for myself these days. I look back at my old fears, pre-Ben, and I shake my head in wonder. What could I have been thinking? Bad clams? Carnival rides? I mean, really—*who cares?* It's so simple now: I don't want Ben to die, and I'm afraid that he will. I hold this fear by the cheeks every day of my life, and I look it right in the face, as bravely and tenderly as I can. It's a funny kind of apotropaic act—as if I can ward off harm by embracing it so boldly. I remember sitting around with a group of other new mothers, way back at the beginning, all of us nursing these tiny beings and kvetching about what needy wretches they were. Eventually, though, one of us would get around to telling a story we'd heard—about a friend whose niece had been diagnosed with leukemia, or about a baby who'd been killed in a car accident—and we'd all clasp our little colicky bundles and weep into their blanketed bodies. We were deranged with sleeplessness and hormones, but it was utterly cathartic. "I'm seriously thinking about having Ben euthanized," I blurted out one day. "I just can't stand worrying about him so much."

These days, I force myself to stay late at work talking to a new friend whose daughter has cystic fibrosis and whose modest wish in life is simply that she outlive him. I drive home. I walk from the car toward our house and I cannot still my imagination: I picture Michael, opening the door with a stricken look on his face. *Something's happened to Ben.* I'm breathless when I arrive, and Ben runs into my arms—this gushing fountain of a toddler, of life itself.

Now we're in the living room with Keith, and Ben is still paralyzed, standing on the rug by Keith's chair. I cross *Bambi* off the mental list of movies I will ever take him to see and wonder what I should say to soothe this frightened boy. I want to promise him that I will never die, but think better of it. Ben finds his own solution instead. He walks over to the Christmas tree, where we have three corny clay gingerbread people hanging, one for each of us, with the words "Mama," "Daddy," and "Ben" painted on them. He gathers the three ornaments from their different places on the tree, holds them in his fist for a moment, and then hangs them all, together, on the same branch. Keith and I don't say a word. I want to tell Ben that it's not his job to keep us all safe, but I reconsider. His magical understanding of the world just might make it feel a little safer for all of us.

Saving Sophie

Erika Schickel

SOPHIE HAS A VOICE LIKE A DIRT ROAD. At three, she sounds like she's been smoking Camel straights for thirty years. It is one of many things I find endearing about her. It is close to dinner time and all the kids are hungry. Sophie (my best friend's daughter and my daughter's best friend) is in the dining room eating some cut-up cantaloupe. It's just a quick snack to save her from melting down before her mom, Rae, takes her and her brother out for dinner. I am in the kitchen, washing the cutting board. In the next room I hear Rae ask her, "Sophie, are you okay? Sophie, are you choking?"

I wait to hear Sophie's husky reply. But Sophie, rarely at a loss for words, is silent. Rae's voice notches up an octave, "Sophie, ARE YOU CHOKING?!"

The word "choking" implies some kind of sound and motion. As I run into the dining room I'm struck by how little of either is coming from Sophie. Her mother scoops her up and pounds her on the back. Nothing. She tries the Heimlich on her daughter, but still Sophie is silent. Choking is a moment of suspended animation; time slows, then quickly wastes.

I, too, give Sophie a whack on the back. This has never not

worked before and we keep hitting and shaking her. Gobs of cantaloupe come flying out of her mouth, but still there is no sound.

As we shake her harder I can tell that this is not going anywhere. We are too unfocused. Precious seconds are ticking past. "Oh my God, what do we do?" Rae pleads, her voice a tightened piano wire of fear. I take Sophie from Rae, who crumples to the floor. The room chills. Death is in here with us and Rae, a fatalist by nature, is accepting it. "Oh God, she's going to die."

Her words strike me as preposterous. *No one is dying here today,* I think as I stick my finger in Sophie's mouth and feel around. I feel her tongue, her palate, her uvula. There is something soft and round at the back of her throat. Is that the melon, or a tonsil? The flesh of both is nearly identical to my sightless fingertip. But this thing is in the wrong place, it's got to be melon. I can touch it, but I can get no purchase on it. I pull my finger out.

What do I do? I don't want to push it further down. Should I stop? Rae has begun keening, letting out an anguished wail. The room grows darker, and I wonder for a moment if this is the shutting down of life as we know it. *No!* I think. *It's late, it's dinner time, it's tubby time. It's time to try again.*

Sophie's jaws are clamped shut. "Open up, Sophie!" I command as I pry her teeth apart and reach in. I touch that soft mound again, and again and again, and I hope this poking at least will cause her to vomit and dislodge the melon. I push my big hand farther into her small mouth, and I extend my finger as far back as it possibly can go and then . . . I feel the tip of my nail dig into the soft flesh of the cantaloupe and I hook it and bring it up.

Sophie's voice escapes in a pained yowl, spit and blood run down her chin and, finally, a red glob like a piece of blood orange drops out of her mouth and lands on top of her pink suede *Blue's Clues* sneaker, which is lying on the floor.

"She's okay!" I announce in a sing-songy voice that I hope will diffuse all our dread. Rae gathers her child up and presses her, gasping, into her body. She holds her as though she'd like to put her right back inside of her, where she knows it's safe. I look up to see my own children, Franny and Georgia, agape and confused, staring at the bloody glob on Sophie's shoe.

"Sophie's bleeding," my own three-year-old daughter observes.

"I must've scratched her throat with my nail," I try to explain. I feel guilty, like I've hurt her friend needlessly. I grab a paper towel and quickly wipe up the evidence of my assault. This is my house, my cantaloupe, my fault. I bring Sophie a damp rag and wipe her face. I get her a drink of cool water. I wonder if Sophie will be afraid of me now. I say again, this time to Rae, "I really had to dig around in there. I'm afraid I scratched her throat with my fingernail."

I think about that fingernail. A lifelong nail biter, I only recently found the self-restraint to let it grow. Just a thin, eighth-of-an-inch crescent of white has grown in over the past week. It dawns on me that if I were still biting my nails, Sophie might have died.

I sit down on the floor. My legs are quivering and can't hold me up. Rae is sitting on the floor, too, and incredibly, she is putting Sophie's shoes on. She promised her kids dinner at Burger King, and if that is still the plan then life must be going on. I am stunned by how quickly we shifted from ordinary, to extraordinary, and then back again. It all happened so fast I wonder if it happened at all. Rae stands Sophie on her feet and shuffles across the floor to me on her knees and throws her arms around me. "Thank you," she says, "thank you for saving my daughter's life."

In terms of drama, saving a life outranks giving life. The miracle of birth is long and logical, dawning on you slowly, so by the time your baby is in your arms, it all seems perfectly right. But saving a life is much different: it is a flash of brinkmanship, an odd mixture of luck, guts, and stubborn denial.

Sophie's father, David, called later to thank me, but the words "thank you" and "you're welcome" belong to the etiquette of everyday life and felt hollow to us both. While he tried to express his gratitude, I tried to reckon with what I'd learned about everyday life: that normalcy is nothing more than a silken curtain that hangs between us and death, which is always in the room. The curtain merely obscures death's presence so we don't lose our minds to fear. It's as though we are living in a perverse episode of *Let's Make a Deal*. At any time Carol Merrill can pull back the curtain to reveal a lifetime's supply of grief. In these moments either the instrument of salvation is on hand and functioning, able to yank the curtain shut again, or it isn't. It all had very little to do with me. In fact, rather than feeling heroic, saving Sophie made me see how truly helpless I am.

For a moment I wondered why we ever take the chance of having children in the first place, when so much is at stake. But then, in the background of David's house, I heard Sophie's gravelly little voice, calling out for her bedtime bottle. We hung up the phone and I went to kiss my own children goodnight.

Passing Clouds

Suzanne Schryver

ON THE WINDOWSILL, a small pot of miniature daffodils bloom, undaunted by the snowstorm raging only inches away. I bought the flowers impulsively on a day when I'd had enough of winter and felt, in some small way, I had control over the arrival of spring.

This winter, barely two weeks old, has not been kind to parents of small children. The last time I took my children out to play, I had to rescue my oldest—just under three-and-a-half-feet tall—from a snow pile by shoveling a path into the middle of the front lawn. When I finally freed him, I had to dig for another five minutes to uncover his buried boot. Today, the blizzard has dumped a foot of fresh snow on top of the eighteen inches that have fallen in the past week. And the weatherman promises nearly another foot in the next twenty-four hours.

It's early January and cabin fever is already hitting us hard. With this incessant storm, we are beginning to feel trapped. I stare at the daffodils, dreaming of spring and warm weather as my two-and-a-half-year-old screams with all the energy her little lungs can muster, drowning out the stereo, the piercing bleeps of the ringing telephone, and the staccato clack of the knife on the wooden cutting board as I chop vegetables for dinner.

The nonstop screams began several minutes earlier in a moment that seemed innocent enough at the time, a potty moment. She announced that she was "done," and when I went to remove her from the potty, she said, "I goed poopy."

"Yes, you did!" I smiled as I handed her a small wad of toilet paper. I helped her wipe, took her off the toilet, and pulled up her underwear and pink-flowered tights. "Flush, and we'll wash your hands."

"I want chocolate M. Go poopy," she told me. During the early potty-training stages, we rewarded each successful session with a single M&M. She trained quickly, and several months later, we were learning that some habits are hard to break. The delectably sweet morsels had cast their wicked spell on my middle child.

"Justine," I responded gently. "You don't need Ms anymore. You know how to go potty."

"I want chocolate M. Go poopy." The words were the same, the emphasis was greater.

I shook my head. "Not now." I stood and walked back to my dinner preparation.

The combination of want and the fatigue of a long day finally took its toll, and this small bundle of child had more feelings than her little body could contain. Justine exploded in a mess of red face and dripping tears in the middle of the once peaceful kitchen. I tried every shred of parenting wisdom—besides giving in—to appease her. Yet the screams continued. And Justine, my only girl, sandwiched tightly between two boys, can scream like no one I've ever encountered.

Now, she stands her ground behind me in the kitchen, demanding attention in a way that is at once completely inappropriate yet totally fitting for her age. If I give in, she will win, learning that this behavior will get her what she wants. And yet, if I continue to ignore her, I will lose. The tirade will continue for too many long minutes. I sigh, rinse my hands, and dry them on the towel.

I turn to find that my daughter's outburst has drawn a crowd. Baby Wesley, who had been happily playing with his Fisher-Price Little People under the kitchen table, now peeks around the corner of the cabinet, his expression one of baby confusion, both worried and amused. Cameron, with the curiosity typical of a four-and-a-half-year-old, watches my reaction, calculating how he might behave in his next moment of want.

I squat to Justine's level. She is oblivious to all that surrounds her, consumed by her tantrum. I take her small, damp hand in mine. "Justine?" The question is meant to penetrate her fury, giving me the quiet spot I need to insert my words. The screams continue. I kneel in front of her, gently taking her face in my hands, guiding her eyes—always brighter blue while she is crying—to mine. Softly, I say, "Quiet. Listen." I put my finger to my lips. Her screams muffle to sobs.

"Come into the family room. Sit with me while you calm down." She clutches her "nappy," an old cloth diaper, and wipes her face in the exaggerated movements common to toddlers. I take her hand and lead her to the couch in the family room. She stands in front of me, refusing the offer of my lap, her sniffles and whines continuing.

"I want a chocolate M," she demands through the sobs that rock her.

"Justine," I shake my head. "I don't get a chocolate M every time I use the potty, do I?" It is reasoning she will not understand.

She shakes her head, her tone rising again. "But I want one!" She stomps her foot on the floor with the word "want."

I pull her onto the couch next to me and, against my best judgment, I turn on the TV and click the TiVo to her favorite program. Within seconds, her sobs quiet to sniffles, and she is drawn in by funny little redheaded Maggie with the map in her hat and her friends Ferocious Beast and Hamilton.

I rise from the couch defeated, kicking myself for resorting to the television to distract my child, and knowing, in some small way, that I've failed by being unable to perform the indomitable task myself. Yet, finally, it is quiet.

Barely an hour after the storm sweeps through our house, dinner is winding down. Justine has finished eating and gotten down to play. She walks around the table to my chair. "I want to get up on your wap."

I reach down and lift her small body onto mine. Instantly, she molds to me, enfolding herself in my arms. I smile at her and she smiles back, showing me her beautiful white baby teeth forced out of line by a lifetime of thumb-sucking. "Rock me like a baby."

I close my eyes and begin to rock, relishing the feel of her warmth, the softness of her skin; memorizing every detail and storing it for the day she doesn't want to be held and cuddled anymore. "Sing!" she commands. Obediently, I begin.

"Rock-a-bye Steeny, on the treetop . . ."

"Baby." She stops me. "Say 'baby,' not 'Steeny'."

I look at her, feigning surprise. "Are you sure that's the way it goes?"
"Yes," she nods with serious certainty. "Sing 'baby.'"
I begin again. "Rock-a-bye girlfriend, on the treetop . . ."
"No!" she giggles. "Say 'baby'!"
Again, I fake my surprise. "Are you sure it's not 'girlfriend'?"
"No! It's baby," she squeals. "Sing!"
"Rock-a-bye baby girl, on the treetop . . ." The exchange continues in the playful manner in which it began. Back and forth we go, me rocking and singing, she correcting my singing errors with her peals of child laughter, which ring through the house.

Night has turned the windows black, allowing us to forget the storm outside. For now, the windows reflect the warmth of the kitchen and the giggling little girl on my lap.

Eye to Eye

Paul Kivel

I LOVED PLAYING WITH ARIEL when he was a baby. He cradled in my arm like my body was meant to hold him. I could carry him easily, close to me, on my stomach in a Snugli, on my back in a backpack, or on my hip. I liked to just sit and feed him a bottle or watch him sleep. I picked him up, held him, moved him about, sat with him all at my level. Occasionally I sat on the floor placing objects within his reach, but most of our time he was up in the air. Of course he let me know when he was uncomfortable but he couldn't really initiate contact. Most of our interactions were on my terms.

So I was quite surprised when he started to toddle about, precariously yet independently. I knew he would eventually learn to walk but I didn't think it would change our relationship so much. He still liked to be carried around on my shoulder or in a backpack sometimes, but mostly he wanted to use his newfound walking ability to explore things at his level. That left me up in the air.

I soon realized that we were operating from different perspectives on the world. He was familiar with mine but I knew little about his. In addition, talking from five feet nine inches aboveground down to him at two-and-a-half feet reasserted my power and control and did not foster the more egalitarian relationship I wanted to build. Neither of us was comfortable with my talking down to him and his resistance to being talked down to was expressed loud and clear.

I decided to stoop to his level. I began to squat to talk with him or gain his attention. But I couldn't stoop for long without feeling awkward and becoming physically uncomfortable. I realized that if I really wanted us to be able to talk and play together, I had to actually sit on the ground, at his level. Just bending over for a minute or squatting awkwardly for a short while before standing again was not going to allow me to really listen to and respond to him.

We set up a play rug and I started spending more time on it. We moved a beanbag chair into the living room so that I could sit comfortably at his height. I didn't start spending all my time on the floor, but I made a conscious effort to be at his level more often and to be more responsive to his desires. He could hug me or climb on me when he wanted to, and we could play games with materials within his reach. Our physical give-and-take was not just at my initiative. I noticed that our time together regained some of the intimacy we had established earlier.

One Saturday morning, when Ariel was playing contentedly by himself, I grabbed the newspaper and sat down on the beanbag chair nearby. It was very satisfying watching him play animatedly with his DUPLOs and I was just as comfortable as I would have been reading the paper at the kitchen table. (I guess that's what they call "parallel play.") Eventually he grew tired of building things, looked up, and noticed me. Next thing I knew, one of his puppets was peeking over the top of my newspaper, looking down on me and inviting me to play. Soon we were creating a story together over the top of the newspaper, which we used like a stage. I had to stop reading the paper in the middle of an article but I knew I could always get back to it later. Besides, the article was much less interesting than the puppet show we created together.

In addition to having fun on the ground, I was surprised by how different the world looked from Ariel's level. The world is more mysterious down there because you can't see around or over things. Objects really do disappear and reappear miraculously. The height of doorknobs and chairs seriously limits access to other places and greater heights. Other people's legs are often curious shapes and occasionally dangerous ones. It is certainly not as easy to get an adult's attention from the level of their knee. These observations gave me a better understanding of Ariel's needs, concerns, and reactions. We had a lot of fun on the floor.

I don't spend much time on the floor now that my children are grown. Less-flexible knees and hips make me reluctant to get down even when I am around toddlers. But I will never lose the insights I gained from that vantage point. I know my relationship with my children shifted in important ways because I could see things from their height. We were able to continue relating to each other with the intimacy of eye-to-eye contact.

Stinky Face

Mary Jane Beaufrand

EVER SINCE MY DAUGHTER HAS BEEN OLD ENOUGH TO WALK, she's been escaping.

As a toddler in music class, she would start each session on my lap, gripping my knees, afraid to bang drums or whack xylophones. I would sit cross-legged and whisper encouragements: *Go on, honey. Make noise.* Then I would sing and airplane her to the dance of the Sugarplum Fairy. I sang with enthusiasm but little skill, hoping she would realize it's okay to sing badly as long as you use your voice. For the most part this worked. By the end of each class she would be cackling wildly, eluding my grasp, and making for things she knew she shouldn't touch: my keys, our instructor's CD player, shoes lined up in perfect rows by the door.

She also escaped at bedtime. After her evening bath her father, Juan, would hoist her out of the tub and wrap her in a mauve bath sheet. After I picked up rubber duckies and stacking cups, I'd find Sofia running naked in our bedroom, looping through the closets, smiling a smug smile. Juan ran after her with a clean diaper, calling, "*¿Para dónde vas, vagabunda?* (Where are you going, you bum?)"

I loved the sound of the word "vagabunda." It made me picture Sofia older, happy, still wildly sprouting curly brown hair. I imagined her brave enough to have adventures, comfortable enough to make mistakes. The kind of girl who doesn't mind getting caught in a twister and plopping herself down on a witch.

After her nightly escape, she always seemed content. Once caught and jammied, she drank her bottle and fondled her satin-edged blanket as I read aloud. Her favorite book was *I Love You, Stinky Face*, about a little boy who tests his mother. "What if I were this way? Or this? Would you still love me?" On each page, the child asks the question and turns into some new strange and nasty thing: a skunk, ape, dinosaur, green alien, slimy swamp monster. With each transformation, the child's mother tags along after him, reasonable and ponytailed, offering exactly what the child needs: hugs, lullabies, piles of hamburgers. No matter how hideous the child, the mother always stays the same: full of treats and love.

When Sofia turned two, she got a present she hadn't asked for and sometimes wished would go back where it came from—a new baby brother.

For a short time—a *very* short time—it looked as though juggling two young children would be easy. Sofia seemed to love Baby Ricky. She hugged and patted him constantly. Occasionally she applied too much pressure when patting him on the head. *Nice baby. Whap whap whap.* Sometimes she shook as she touched him, as if the pressure of not being able to whack him repeatedly was enough to induce a seizure.

Everything seemed fine until Ricky turned yellow.

The color traveled from his head down the length of him. It was as if some invasive vine had taken hold and was spreading yellow tendrils all over his small body. Nothing turned it back.

A nursing service installed a baby tanning bed for his jaundice. The bed came with what looked like a Members Only jacket, the back of which opened to expose Ricky's skin to the lights. We had to strap him into this atrocity and leave him there for the better part of the day. Holding and feeding him? That was fine—but only at three-hour intervals. Even that was measured: I had to chart how long he nursed, how often he pooped, and what color the poop was: yellow, brown, or green. I moved his tanning bed from the nursery to the master bedroom so I could hear him better, even if all I could do was listen. Sometimes I wanted to pick him up so badly I thought *I* would have a seizure from the self-restraint.

My mother came to stay with us while the baby recovered and my C-section incision healed. I let her take care of Sofia. My mother is more than capable, so I thought everything outside the jaundice room was fine. It wasn't.

Every morning, when I came downstairs for breakfast, I would sit with Sofia and her granny and have my morning bagel and Percocet. Sometimes I got through three bites before Ricky started crying and I leapt up, combat-ready. The instant I turned my back on my daughter, she started crying as well. "No, Mommy, no!" Her lower lip would jut out and huge tears splashed into her Cheerios. Sometimes I let Ricky cry, and sat an anxious five minutes with Sofia, trying to calm her but needing to go. Then I would disappear back into our room, where everything seemed dull and cloying; every object yellow, brown, or green. I heard my daughter as I mounted the stairs, wailing and disconsolate. Then I heard my own mother, prying Sofia's fists from the baby gate at the foot of the stairs. "Stop it, honey, you're making Granny tired."

Suddenly, the little things Sofia did no longer seemed charming. Her nightly escape, for example. Not only did she have to bathe alone, but there was no one to follow her as she did her naked laps around the bedroom. "Sofi," Juan would say wearily, "I don't have time for this," and neatly close the closet door, trapping her on one side. After a while she stopped running completely. Instead she'd blankly stare at the TV as we forced one limp foot then the other into her jammies.

My mother went home, spent from caregiving. My incision healed. Ricky's face took on a rosy color; the tanning bed was sent back with the nurses. By this time I too was careworn. It showed in my face and the way I would pull out of a Starbucks parking lot with my latte still on my sunroof.

It didn't matter. I looked forward to a new equilibrium; I wanted to savor my new family. But that took practice. Sofia's father took her to music class now. I'd stopped going when I was too pregnant to airplane her. And now that I was strong enough to sing and dance, I didn't want to. Instead, I spent hours on the sofa watching *Star Trek* reruns with Ricky in my arms. *There is no way,* I thought, *I am ever putting this baby down again.*

Meanwhile, Sofia was learning more words, mostly things she wanted . . . or didn't. "I don't want to go to the store. I don't want Mommy coffee. I don't want to hold your hand. I want animal crackers. I want a bath. Not that story, this one. I don't want to go to bed." And she repeated her demands incessantly. Pizza. Crackers. Juice. Playground. No. No. No.

One day when Ricky was four months old and the sun was shining, I loaded the kids into a double stroller and we went to the park. On the way home, Sofia got bored. Her crackers had run out. The juice had run out. Soon, she was throwing herself around in the stroller, arching her back and running her hands over the grimy wheels. My arms were tired from pushing the stroller uphill. I'd left my latte under the swings. The only thing I could think of was to distract her. So I started to sing. "The ants go marching . . ."

"No, Mommy, no!" she said.

There was no mistaking her command, but I ignored her. These days Sofia said no to everything.

I kept going: ". . . one by one, hurrah . . ."

"No, Mommy, no!" she repeated.

I tried another song. And another. And another. She rejected every one. Finally we reached home.

The next Saturday we were in the car on the way to the beach— a one-hour trip, including the ferryboat crossing—and Sofia dropped her pacifier in the backseat. "I want my binky. Where binky go? Where binky go?" she cried. I couldn't retrieve it without pulling over. I didn't want to pull over. We had a boat to catch.

"I don't know," I answered. Then: "There it is, on the floor." And finally, a half-hour later: "I don't know. Shut up shut up *shut up!*"

I tried again to use music to distract her. I played her favorite *Jungle Book* CD. When Baloo started singing "Bare Necessities," I sang along with him. From the backseat, I heard it again: "No, Mommy, no."

I'd been listening to her working herself into a tantrum all morning. I was tired. "Damn it, Sofia, I can sing if I want to." I turned up the volume and sang along with Baloo, loudly, even though she kept repeating, "No, Mommy, no!" louder and louder until she was screaming and giant tears coursed down her face.

When we reached the beach, where Juan was waiting for us, Sofia was puffy and red and residual sniffles quaked her whole body. "You take her," I told my husband, and went back to the car to cuddle the baby.

Two days later, I was fixing breakfast when she started singing "Old MacDonald Had a Farm." Without thinking, I joined in.

"And on this farm he had some cows . . ."

"No, Mommy, no."

I buried my face in my hands. It was only nine-thirty in the morning.

"Enough!" I said, and shoved her bananas and cereal in front of her. "I will sing if I want to. Do you understand?"

"No, Mommy, no!"

"E-I-E-I-O!" I walked through the house picking up toys, doing the dishes, folding the laundry, and singing loudly. "With a quack quack here!"

She tailed after me yelling, "No, Mommy, no!"

Sorting the day's mail, I slammed the pile of bills on the dining room table and stopped singing. Sofia stopped shouting. I stood there for a second, savoring the silence between us. Then I had a revelation.

"I drown you out, don't I, vagabunda?" I asked.

Even though I knew she didn't understand what it meant, to drown out, for the first time since I'd brought her brother home, she said "yes."

Her favorite story is wrong, that one with the child testing the mother. Part of it rang true: in four months my child had changed from toddler to ape to dinosaur to alien to swamp monster. But with each of Sofia's ugly transformations, I too had changed, into something bigger and stinkier.

I didn't like this revelation. I had gotten through the past months assuming *she* was the bratty one and I was coping as best I could. But I was wrong. Then I blamed Sofia. *Look at what you've made me become,* I thought. *I used to be good at this.* But that feeling quickly passed. Then I felt even sadder.

That morning I realized that toddlerhood is just a stage she would grow out of, a transformation from which she would emerge a regular child. But I knew I would never make it back to being that storybook mother. There would always be times when Sofia would shirk my hand as we crossed the street and I would grip it harder. There would be times when I couldn't retrieve her binky from where she threw it on the car floor. Worse, there would be times when I would say "yes" just because she said "no."

I stood there, looking at my daughter, her curly hair a halo of brown question marks. She watched me, waiting for something she didn't think she would get. But I loved her for demanding it.

"You're right. I'll be quiet now."

Then there it was, that smug vagabunda grin I used to love. She turned away from me and began her escape.

"Moo moo. Quack quack." She galloped around the house, alternately cackling wildly and making farm animal noises. "Baa baa. Woof woof."

Even if I wasn't the ponytailed reasonable mother from *I Love You, Stinky Face,* I knew that at some point Sofia and I would learn to sing together again. But not now. Now it was *her* turn. In that moment, it was enough to listen to her filling the house with music, finding her own voice.

Is It Day Now?

Shu-Huei Henrickson

WE SMELT THE MOSSY WET SOIL and heard the stubborn quiet patter on the windowpanes while eating leftover pot stickers for breakfast. I looked out at the sullen sky as Guai Guai shouted, "I want candy, Mama, I want candy." Rain was not supposed to start this early.

I had hoped Guai Guai and I could go to the riverside bike path before it started to rain. He woke up screaming for his pretend pork chops: spatulas, ladles, and wooden spoons masquerading as meat. Nothing I did could console him. I had to walk away telling him to calm his contorted two-and-a-half-year-old self down *by himself.*

We had already had a difficult start this Sunday morning. The rain would make it harder. Where could we go?

We had gone to the mall the day before. The science museum is closed on Sundays. The playgrounds would be wet. Our recent trip to the bookstore resulted in Guai Guai's pulling books off shelves after three minutes inside. I didn't feel like visiting the neighbors.

It wouldn't be true to say we had absolutely nowhere to go. We could visit the mall again. Guai Guai loved escalators, coffee shops (where he charmed the teenagers at the counter by asking for a cup of water, please), the small indoor playground, the food court, and the garbage cans (he often peeked in to see how full they were). We could go to a restaurant and order a piece of pie, just to have something to do.

The truth was I didn't want to go anywhere. I wished I were by myself. When Guai Guai asked me to play his favorite Raffi CD, I taught him how to push the PLAY button and tried not to seem impatient. His exotic half-Asian, half-Caucasian eyes looked engaging and serious when he pointed at the right button, "This one?" He played the CD all day, and I tried in vain to exorcise the haunting Raffi songs from my head. I told myself I needed time to write. I had all these story and essay ideas, but I didn't have the time and the peace of mind to write them. I wished Guai Guai's father wasn't away at a conference this weekend.

But I also knew that when I had tasks I needed to accomplish in the past, I often wanted to do something else. I wanted to crochet when I had a graduate paper due. I wanted to write when I had student papers to mark. I wanted to exercise when I had a meeting to attend. I wanted to read when I finally had time to write. Guai Guai was my responsibility, and I hankered for time alone.

Desperate to keep Guai Guai occupied, I gave him a bath, twelve hours after his previous one. He loved water so much that a bath would keep him busy for an hour. While he took his bath, I sat on the toilet reading Mary Morris's *Nothing to Declare: Memoirs of a Woman Traveling Alone*. I normally sat next to the tub talking and playing with him, but I just didn't feel like being close to him. Guai Guai did not demand my attention; he was happy to be swimming, as he put it, "with his wee wee."

While reading, I couldn't stop fiddling with my bookmark—a boarding pass from a recent trip, London Heathrow to Washington Dulles. Testaments to my wanderlust, boarding passes are my favorite bookmarks. I always plot my next trip before getting home from the current one. As I caressed the boarding pass between my thumb and forefinger, I suddenly realized, with horror, that worse than my habitual, nagging avoidance behavior remained the thought that I wished I didn't have Guai Guai at all.

I wished I didn't have family responsibilities and pressures. I longed to be alone again. The thought of having to get to know my child's friends' parents after he started school made me cringe. When I accused Guai Guai's father of not being helpful, when I became frustrated with Guai Guai's tantrums, I was in fact wishing to be free, thinking about the overseas job postings E-mailed to me every Friday. I wanted to be a woman traveling alone, like Morris, but not because of Morris. I had already had these longings when I wandered away from my first husband. I wanted to join the Peace Corps. I dreamt of living and working in exotic places. I wanted freedom of movement.

I was frightened by this realization: I was unfit to be a mother.

I couldn't possibly articulate this thought to anybody. Any responsible person would be more disturbed than I by my horrible thoughts. They would not believe me if I told them that despite these longings I truly loved Guai Guai, more than anybody in this world, more than I loved my parents, more than I loved Guai Guai's father.

But, I suppose, not more than I loved myself.

• • •

Is It Day Now?

Guai Guai came unbidden. When the pregnancy test proved positive, I felt a seditious sense of pleasure. Being single, I wasn't supposed to be happy to find myself pregnant. I had been divorced less than a year, and I hadn't yet figured out how to announce the divorce to my parents. While telling my colleagues and friends that I was pregnant, I felt like I had to put on a sad face. I couldn't concoct a rational reason why a woman like me, always wanting to wander, should have a baby.

Yet I fancied the idea of being a successful single mom. My child would be bilingual as soon as he was born. He would speak perfect Chinese and English. Later, he would pick up French, German, and Japanese with ease. He would sit, civilized, at the dinner table and in restaurants, unlike my sister's spoiled little thing. He would not scream or misbehave on airplanes. I would take him everywhere with me. He would be so easy, so perfect.

Guai Guai's father wanted to be involved. We became euphoric partners. The arrival of Guai Guai was the most important thing in the universe, and the whole world stopped to witness the birth of our love child. We couldn't understand how other people could be satisfied with their children when they saw what a beautiful baby we had. We would hold hands gawking at Guai Guai sleeping in his crib. We thought raising a child was as simple as we had anticipated. Eventually, we transformed our commuting partnership into a commuting marriage.

That was when Guai Guai slept most of the time.

Guai Guai no longer takes naps, and he has opinions now. Too many of them. After his bath, he had to dry himself off, put his diaper on standing up, put his shorts on sitting down, and he couldn't possibly wear a sweatshirt. When he didn't want me to help him with something, he yelled, "No, Mama! Stop it, Mama!" When I asked him to bring his favorite Moo Moo to bed, he pouted, "It is somebody else's cow."

I bragged about Guai Guai's language proficiency, about how Guai Guai spoke in complete sentences, how he used the past tense correctly most of the time, how he knew about simple conjunctions and dependent clauses, how he thought in terms of analogies ("Look it, Mama, it's a carrot," as he discovered himself on the potty).

But I didn't tell people how taxing it was sometimes to have such a communicative child. Wouldn't it be easier if he would just do what I wanted him to, if he said "yes" some of the time, if he wasn't so contrary?

After his bath, we looked through pictures of our travels in Germany, England, Taiwan, and pictures of Guai Guai at different stages of cuteness. My favorite was of him sleeping in his car seat, buckled down in a confined space, safe, peaceful, and, above all, quiet. No threat of him talking back at me. No threat of him scattering toys all over the floors, breaking the TV antenna, drawing on the walls, bending my CDs with his greasy fingers, or soaking the carpet with milk.

After the pictures, I asked Guai Guai to help make an avocado wrap. He stood on a chair next to me at the kitchen counter. I began by spreading a thin layer of mayonnaise on a large tortilla. He ran his fingers over the mayonnaise and delighted in licking up the white fat.

"Don't use any spinach, Mama, I don't like spinach," he demanded. "More tomatoes, Mama, more tomatoes . . . do you have to have pine nuts on our sandwich, Mama? They're too crunchy . . . what is *that* in the middle of the avocado?"

"That's called a stone, *hsi-tow,* Guai Guai. We'll put this half of the avocado away with the stone in it. We'll leave the *hsi-tow* in, so the avocado won't turn brown."

"We'll leave the *hsi-tow* in, so the avocado won't turn brown," Guai Guai repeated after me.

I thumbed the brown hard stone and wondered whether it would really prevent the green avocado from oxidizing. A friend, who introduced me to the avocado, taught me that trick a long time ago. I always used up the leftover half right away. I never tried to see how long the stone would keep the avocado green or if the avocado would really turn without the stone. Was the stone the baby of the avocado? Would the baby keep the mother from turning brown? Or was the stone the mother? I was thinking too much.

Guai Guai put the leftover avocado away while I rolled up our wrap. Guai Guai liked to share food. We ate on the porch swing and watched the drizzle.

As usual, Guai Guai wouldn't sit still for very long. He ran down the steps into the yard and looked up at the sky with his mouth wide open. "I'm drinking the rain, Mama."

I felt worse about my restlessness, about wanting to be alone. This child took pleasure in such simple things.

The rain had stopped by the time we finished our lunch. The sky looked less gray, less sullen. Guai Guai opened the glass door to the house and closed the screen door instead.

"I'm letting the breeze into the house, Mama."

Yes, the breeze. Sitting on the porch, I could feel it too. I walked down the yard to see if I could find a rainbow. It would be nice to talk to Guai Guai about the rainbow.

"What are you looking at, Mama?"

I didn't see the rainbow.

"The sun, Guai Guai, I'm looking for the *tai-yang*."

"Where is the *tai-yang*, Mama?"

"It's hiding, but I think it will come out soon."

Perhaps the sun would come out for a few hours before night. Perhaps we could go to the bike path for a little while.

"Is it day now, Mama?" Guai Guai asked. He smiled up at me, drawing slanting lids across his round, dark brown eyes.

After the Fall

James di Properzio

I WAS THE BEST FATHER. I was fortunate enough to be a full-time dad, with work I could do from home. My wife's job as a professor took her out of the home only a few hours a week, so our daughter had, essentially, two full-time parents. I bent all my efforts to giving her the best care and food, the most loving attention, the most intellectually stimulating play any baby had ever had. I was the fastest cloth-diaper changer east of the Mississippi. My baby was the most intelligent, inquisitive, healthy, affectionate toddler ever to toddle. She had my ears, my hair, my large head and high brow—beautiful. We made our own organic baby food out of whole grains, kale, broccoli, kelp, and brewer's yeast; we washed our diapers without toxic detergents or bleach; kept our daughter away from mercury-preserved vaccines. Hesperus thrived.

Then we took her to France. At seventeen months, she was speaking French, watching Guignol in puppet shows, singing Renaissance toccatas, running around the Champs-de-Mars playgrounds. The penultimate day of our two-week stay, we decided to take the Metro to the Paris Aquarium.

We had bought an umbrella stroller during our visit—the best! European-made, ergonomic, safety-tested—since we only had a running stroller at home. Jennifer grabbed some *fruits biologiques* from the apartment while I got Hesperus ready and brought her down the hall so she could reach up and press the elevator button. We wheeled her down the narrow sidewalks to the Dupleix Metro station. I fumbled some tickets out of my pocket while pushing the stroller with one hand, gave one to Jennifer, and held another in my teeth like some kind of pirate dad.

When the passageway bottlenecks at the turnstiles, the flow of Parisians just accelerates to make up for the increased density. Many thoughtful commuters were speeding things up by hurdling the turnstiles and skipping altogether the time-consuming second it takes to validate a ticket. They still had to shoulder aside the swinging barrier, like the saloon door in a spaceship, that provides no additional security while making the process more cumbersome for everyone. Rather than stop and try to hold my position against the torrent while getting Hesperus out of the stroller, I picked her up stroller and all and walked through, saying "Whee! Flying!" I side-stepped through the turnstiles with her and put my shoulder to the steel saloon door. The door put up a struggle, and I didn't want it to bang her knees, so I lifted her high over the door, above my head. The door swung open sixty degrees and stopped. I leaned forward to shove free past it, looking up to make sure Hesperus stayed secure in her three-point harness. As the stroller tilted above me, I saw her lean, peering curiously at the ground, the straps dangling loose where I had forgotten to fasten them. She fell.

After the Fall

Headfirst, eyes widening, she tumbled inverted past me as I let the stroller fall away and threw myself against the barrier separating us. I passed it as she hit the concrete flat on her back and the back of her head. She goggled up at me, winded and bewildered, as I screamed for my wife, screamed that she fell, and screamed it again. Hesperus wailed. I crouched beside her, touching her but paralyzed for fear of hurting her further if her neck or back were broken. My wife swept past me and snatched her up, holding her close and walking her to calm her. I watched from where I knelt as my wife and daughter walked away from me up a dingy staircase to another of the concrete slabs held apart by the girders of the grim Metro station.

I remember commuters scurrying past without a glance, hopping turnstiles, hurrying indifferently on to their business, like rats in the walls. The father I had been for seventeen months crouched broken there, in that dirty, industrial, and uncaring place. Never in the intense emotions of childhood, not when my grandfather died, never had I felt the loss of something so precious. That is the one moment when my life stopped, the world I had built cracked, and I stopped being who I was and had wanted to be. I let her fall.

I collected the stroller and looked for them, took the stairs three at a time, pulling out a borrowed cell phone. Hesperus was sniffling and saying "Boom!" every few seconds.

"I'm calling the hospital—do they have ambulance service?—I know there's an American Hospital . . ."

"She's fine, James."

"Boom!"

"Fine? We have to get her checked out."

"She cried right away, now she's over it, she's not bleeding or acting funny; she's fine."

"Boom!"

"Let's just go to the aquarium, James. I think you need to hold her and see she's all right. Here comes the train."

I held her to me more nervously and gingerly than when she was first born. "Hesperus, are you okay, sweetheart?"

"Boom!"

"I know, you went boom, I'm so sorry. Should we go see some fishies?" She nodded enthusiastically. "Does anything hurt you?"

"Boom!"

I stroked her back, surreptitiously feeling for breaks or sore spots. There were none. The train pulled up to the quay. She hugged my shoulder, muttering "boom" into my deltoid, and I held her head against me. It wasn't her head. There was a hole, no break in the skin, just a depressed crater the size of my thumb on the back of her smooth, round, familiar skull.

I told my wife to feel it. She blanched. The train pulled away.

We rushed down to a cab and spent an agonized hour in traffic to get to the American Hospital. In the waiting room Hesperus played calmly and happily with the toys. The French doctor was calm and gentle. He listened with concern as Jennifer explained that Hesperus had fallen from a height of a meter and a half.

"*Deux mètres,*" I corrected. I had said a meter and a half in the first place, unable to admit, even to myself, that I had dropped her from a height of two meters—six feet, seven inches.

She had landed on her back, Jennifer told him, on the cement in the Metro. *"Dans le Métro?"* he interrupted, as if this detail were of especial importance. He felt the back of her head with his gentle, tobacco-stained fingers. He went out to bring a second doctor in.

"Elle a quel âge?" the second asked while feeling the back of her head.

"Quinze mois . . . non, dix-sept," Jennifer corrected her addition.

The doctors looked at each other. *"Bien sûr, à dix-sept mois la fontanelle postérieure doit être déjà fermée."*

"Elle est tombée d'une hauteur d'un mètre et demi . . ."

"Deux mètres," I interjected.

"De deux mètres dans le Métro . . ."

"Dans le Métro?" the second doctor interrupted.

Our doctor finished the details, and they agreed that she had none of the usual head trauma symptoms: no vomiting, dilated pupils, loss of consciousness. She was acting normally, but they recommended a scan to see if there was internal damage. Our doctor phoned the neurology unit of the Hôpital Necker to be sure they could see her immediately. I heard the doctor say, *"J'ai ici une toute petite américaine . . . Elle est tombée d'une hauteur de deux mètres, dans le Métro."* Then there was a lot of French I didn't understand, except for the words *"fracture"* and *"balle de ping-pong."* When we paused on our way out to pay his receptionist, he said, in English, "No, don't lose time. It's more important to go now than to give me money."

We took another cab to the premier children's hospital in France. The Hôpital Necker's graven stone gate dates from the French Revolution, but once inside everything is state of the art, and they ushered us in immediately. Two nurses wound my daughter with bandages to a papoose board to immobilize her for the scan, leaving only her terrified face exposed, and one tiny hand that I had requested to hold. She was exhausted and crying hoarsely, red eyes darting in her fixed head. No one had treated her this way since the hour she was born, when she was taken to the nursery to be bathed and have medicines stuck in her eyes and needles jabbed into her foot, where I followed so that she could clutch my finger and hear my voice as she had heard it each day singing and talking to her in utero.

Jennifer, who was pregnant, left the room in tears with the nurses.

They slid Hesperus into the CT scanner, a sleek massive chrome ring standing obliquely in an empty white chamber. I bent into the machine with her and looked into her face so that she saw me rather than the orbiting Xray gun and told her I was staying with her, that I knew she was scared but that everything was going to be okay. I sang to her over the palpable hum as it bathed us in an invisible and poisonous light. She quieted, her reddened eyes still frightened but latched onto me for comfort as firmly as her hand on my finger.

Afterward I wandered discreetly into the neurosurgeon's viewing room and looked up at the cutaway shots of my daughter's skull, ovals of such perfect symmetry that they seemed constructions of pure geometry and light rather than a growing formation of several fused bones. Each was different in size but similar in shape, a tapering cross-section like that of my own large, ovoid skull. But not there, toward the middle of the set, where the largest meridians of her skull cracked at the back, then flattened the perfect curve, the next picture bowing in the back like a time-lapse sequence of the concrete pushing in her skull. I walked out and tried not to think about it, tried to hope it was someone else's, that her bump was in the soft tissue only, that the perfect sphere of my world could remain intact.

The Tunisian neurosurgeon was melancholy. When, as a teenager, I told my doctor I wanted to be a neurosurgeon, he responded that in all his years in medicine he had never met a neurosurgeon who wasn't depressed. The Tunisian said that the occipital bone was fractured. There was no bleeding, fluids, or bruising, no damage to the brain. "Is it pressing on the brain?" I asked, pointing to asymmetry in the ghostly-pale brain—faint and fragile structures where vision is born of the firings of rods and cones and assembled into our picture of the world, like the image at the back of a camera obscura. I played dumb. I wasn't asking what would be wrong; I was asking him to say that all was right.

"Yes," he replied sternly, meaning that he knew I could see it was so. He stared at me as if awaiting any further obvious questions or self-indulgent fantasies, waiting for me to accept reality.

"Will it affect development?" I persevered.

"Too early to tell." He advised us to get her scanned every month for six months, to monitor the fracture.

We went back to the apartment our friend had lent us and put Hesperus to bed. "She's fine," my wife reassured me. "We should have gone to the aquarium."

I was restless and wrung out, unable to make anything of it, waiting for a resolution. "James," Jennifer told me, "You're the one who explained to me that the skull has evolved to do that, to absorb the energy of the impact and save the brain from it, because to learn to walk erect you have to take a lot of falls." But Jennifer couldn't stop the worry, the guilt, the snapshot before my mind's eye of the instant Hesperus hit the concrete.

We flew home the next day. We saw more pediatricians, a neurologist, and finally another neurosurgeon. Jennifer grew raggedly impatient of the process; she knew Hesperus was fine and would be fine, but each visit held up our daughter's fate to fresh scrutiny and made her worry again, if only for a day. But I wasn't satisfied. The doctors could not see any problem but were not sure.

By the time we were in the American neurosurgeon's office, Jennifer had had enough, and was furious at even the brief wait. She glanced crossly around at the diplomas and awards on the walls, the picture on the desk of a woman with big blond hair. "Look at that trophy wife!" she exclaimed. "I'll bet he's got short-guy complex— his diplomas are too high up on the walls."

A few minutes later, a diminutive and lively Middle Eastern man burst through the door with an apprentice in his wake, introduced himself in a heavy Boston accent, and held the Parisian scanner slide up to the light, glancing at it for theatrical effect, since he had obviously just studied it for several minutes. "It's cosmetic!"

"Cosmetic?"

"It's cosmetic. It's not actually touching the brain, there's no damage inside the skull, and there's no bone hanging loose. She'll be fine. If it was on the front of her skull—so it'd look like an ashtray in her forehead—I might operate, but just so kids wouldn't make fun of her. In the back, it's like not anyone'll ever see it—unless she decides to shave her head when she's a teenager. And even then, it probably won't look much different from any other lumpy skull. This kind of thing happens to everyone as a toddler, you just don't know about it 'cause you don't bother to get a CT scan. If you were on a farm in the Midwest you wouldn't have gotten a CT scan, you wouldn't even know it was fractured, and it wouldn't make any difference. Here . . ." he bowed deeply toward Jennifer, seized her hand, and drew it onto the back of his head. "Feel that?"

"Yeah . . ." she said with bemusement and distaste. "What is it?"

He craned his neck to face her. "Who knows? I must've fractured it as a kid. We all have 'em."

That was the last word on it: "cosmetic," like a pimple, or a nose job. For a couple of weeks, whenever we told people we had been in Paris, Hesperus chimed in, "Paris—Boom!" Everyone kept feeling the dent at the back of her head and saying, "Oh, it's definitely getting smaller," but it hasn't, and it doesn't need to. I thought she had forgotten all about it, until yesterday when I asked her while crossing the street to the playground if she remembered Paris. "Hesperus fall down Paris, have boo-boos, need Band-Aid," she responded—and pointed to the fresh scrape on her knee.

Under My Skin

Yvette Bonaparte

"Mommy, look, look."

We have just pulled up in front of my son's preschool, and I am busy untangling him from his car seat.

"You're the same color as him," Liam points frantically out the window. I turn, my mind on other things, and see who my son is pointing at—a man dressed in the familiar gray and orange uniform of the Sunset Scavenger Company. The garbage man. I smile, not quite sure how to react. "Yes, sweetie, I am the same color as him. I'm dark brown and he's dark brown."

"Yes," my three-year-old says proudly, as if he's just finished a jigsaw puzzle all by himself, and we hold hands and walk across the street to his preschool. Once inside, he spies some LEGO trains, his hand slips from my grasp, and he's gone to play with his friends. I stand and watch him, one of only three beige faces among his white school friends and white teachers. I am suddenly acutely aware that I am the only Black mother in a school of eighty families. My husband is Caucasian, and there are a few other biracial families here at the school, mostly Asian-Caucasian.

The only person Liam sees on a regular basis who looks like me is the garbage man.

I have nothing against garbagemen. And my son *is* three. He notices even the smallest details. In the middle of singing, "Twinkle, twinkle, little spaghetti, how I wonder when you'll be ready," he tells me that I have the same shoes as the preschool's director, and asks me what that sesame seed is doing on the floor. The second the avocado seed on the kitchen counter sprouts, Liam pulls me over to see it. He spots everything from the tiniest ladybug in the crack of the sidewalk to the kitten asleep on the neighbor's windowsill.

Although I admire Liam's enthusiasm for the mundane, I want him to notice something more important. I want Liam to realize there are astronauts, teachers, doctors, Nobel Prize winners, and friends who are the same color I am. I want him to notice it so much that he doesn't notice it at all. I want Liam to grow up and be one of many children of color in his school, not the only one. I want him to walk down the street, turn on the television, open a newspaper, scan magazine racks, just be in this world and see many different races. I want him to have a childhood that is more integrated than isolated. But my son seems to think I'm a rarity, and sometimes I do too.

At playgrounds, I see no other Black mothers with their children. At church, I am one of three Black congregants. At museums, I rarely see other Black parents.

When Liam was eighteen months old, I tired of being the only dark face at the weekly play group. I decided to find other Black mothers with whom I could feel a sense of familiarity—moms I could talk to about whether to dread or two-strand-twist my hair, moms with whom I could share anecdotes of the lives of our children.

One friend's daughter recently started attending a new preschool mid-year. A four-year-old white classmate told her at the end of her first day, "I didn't like you when you first came to school because your skin is brown, but now I think you're okay." My friend's usually animated daughter came home subdued and sad, and my friend had to explain to her that there was nothing wrong with having brown skin. The next day, she went with her daughter to talk to the teacher about how the school handles these kinds of incidents. "Oh, that never happened," the teacher told her. "I would have heard it if it had, and I know that girl would never have said that."

I wanted to talk with mothers who had to deal with these issues and others like them. So I posted to a popular local on-line board. The only responses I got were from mothers who wondered why I wanted to separate myself and my child from other mothers and children on the basis of race. I never responded. Why try to explain that we were already separate?

I grew up in a suburb of New Jersey where, for the most part, the only Black people in my apartment building were the Caribbean maids and the men who brought our car around when we called down for it. I went to a private elementary school and a private high school where I was one of two Black children in a class of twenty-five students, and later when I transferred to a parochial school my junior year, mine was the only Black face in the yearbook for the senior class. I rarely saw people in my own image, not classmates, not teachers, not school friends.

"We value diversity," the administrators told me when we applied for preschool admission. They proved it by accepting my son's last-minute application ahead of the applications other families had submitted nearly a year earlier.

Now, I watch Liam with his LEGO trains and wonder if I am making a mistake sending him to a preschool like this one, in a city like this one, in a world like this one. But as I go out the door, the Asian mail carrier smiles at me and slips the mail through the slot. The Black garbageman makes his way up the street with his white partner. I envy my son's ability to be in the present moment, say something, and move on to the next thing. My son is happy, so happy in his preschool that he asks to go on weekends. When I tell him stories about outer space at bedtime, he insists that the planets be named after his teachers: Planet Judith, Planet Kate, and Planet Banette—he can't say Lynette, and I don't correct him.

I also don't correct him when he refers to things as being upside up. He'll figure it out soon enough. Until then, maybe I don't need to do anything. Maybe, just for today, my son can just be an ever-observant, sharp-eyed three-year-old, free of all of my racial baggage, baggage I hope he never picks up.

Deconstructing Little Boys

Gordon Korman

A YEAR OR SO AGO, my friend, Sam, and I were discussing *Thomas the Tank Engine.* (Sad but true: our conversations used to center on Knicks games and the NASDAQ-100, now it's an island of talking trains.) He was complaining that Thomas and his roundhouse clan are a self-absorbed neurotic bunch, obsessed only with new coats of paint and who gets to pull the big express. What kind of an example is that for our kids?

Another friend, Nick, spoke up. "What's *Thomas the Tank Engine?*"

We stared at him, but there was a perfectly rational explanation for his cultural illiteracy. Yes, he had kids, just as we did. But his were *girls.*

The nature-versus-nurture thing had never been much of a debate with me. I was a nurture guy, dyed-in-the-wool, and not just because I generally found myself on the liberal side of most arguments. To me, nurture just made more sense. A newborn baby is a clean slate. Granted, elements of personality are with us from the start, but to make a generalization on the order of "Boys enjoy *this;*

girls enjoy *that*" seemed crazy. Sure, none of us zap our sons with an electric cattle prod whenever they happen to reach for the Barbies, but there must be clues, subliminal signs we give off that communicate the message: "This is not for you. Stay away."

I believed this until the birth of my own son. Despite a painstakingly gender-neutral collection of toys, from the very beginning, Jay has demonstrated an unmitigated attraction to large motorized pieces of equipment. As a one-year-old, his first word was "car." This led to "bus," "truck," "fire truck," and finally to the mother lode that awaits all little boys at the local construction site: "bulldozer," "front loader," "dump truck," "backhoe," "cement-mixer," and "forklift."

At his eighteen-month check-up, the pediatrician inquired as to the size of his vocabulary. Could it be, perhaps, thirty words? At that point Jay knew at least that many terms for heavy equipment alone. He could spot a road grader, obscured by dense foliage, from two hundred yards away, and could name every engine in the local firehouse. If you thought grad school was tough, try facing Jay's look of bewildered disapproval when you fail to distinguish between a turntable ladder engine and a fire rescue truck.

It's perfectly natural that the books and videos that capture his attention are the ones that feature cars and trains—a fact that has not been lost on the publishers in this country. In the children's book section of Barnes & Noble there are more smiles on the vehicles than on the Homo sapiens, more talking modes of transportation than chipmunks. That's little boyhood in the third millennium.

Certainly there's nurture at work too. We live in the New York area, and frequently spend time looking for parking on congested streets. This is not lost on Jay, who constructs massive garages out of wooden blocks and proceeds to park hundreds of miniature cars inside. This with pretty fair approximations of parking-speak: "Do I have enough room back there, Daddy?" or "Do you think we can find a spot?" He backs up his Little Tikes car, peering over his shoulder with his arm across the seat-back. I think to myself, *Nice form. I wonder if I look this good driving in reverse.* Kids emulate what they see their parents doing or have I got that backwards? These days, when I parallel park, it's Jay I visualize, not the guy from the driver's ed. video.

I ran into Nick recently, and he said, "You know, I was watching *Bob the Builder* the other day, and I thought, 'What a bunch of wimps these trucks are. Whoever heard of a crane who's afraid of heights?'"

Didn't I mention it? There's a new baby in Nick's house. A boy.

Love Bites

Marian Brown Sprague

"TOE-BYE." The words, uttered with explosive vehemence from the other side of the room, sounded incongruous coming out of my two-year-old's mouth. I was on the phone with my sister-in-law, Janice. Through the optical fibers that connect Washington, D.C., and Woodside, California, she heard Caroline's words, and the force with which they were pronounced. I explained that she'd been saying this a lot—always in that tone of voice. "Perhaps she's saying 'Tubby,' as in Teletubbies," Janice offered. Maybe. But something in the way Caroline spewed out the words was defiantly out of character.

At two, Caroline was an avid talker. She sang her ABCs with off-key enthusiasm and made easy conversation with the many adults in her life. With near-perfect diction, she would tell anyone who cared to listen about the wild monkeys she'd fed each evening on a recent trip to Barbados, or invite the listener to join her and her imaginary friend, Dannyo, for tea. That was why, try as I might, I couldn't quite accept the Teletubbies explanation. "Toe-bye" was too far removed from "Tubby" to work for me.

Caroline, an only child, had always been amiable and

amenable—a good thing since our advancing age had sapped much of our energy. We traversed the toddler terrain with apparent ease, despite having warily donned suits of armor in preparation for this difficult phase. To our great surprise, and relief, there was nary a tantrum. Even potty training went off without much difficulty. We bid a fond farewell to diapers when she was twenty-five months old. Caroline preferred quiet, dramatic play—spending countless hours orchestrating the dialogue of the family inhabiting her doll house— to the ceaseless climbing and running that slowly erodes a parent's enthusiasm for chasing after a toddling two-year-old. She didn't shove, grab, or hit other children.

Instead, she bit me—timing her attacks carefully, waiting for those most tender of moments when I was holding her close. With the stealth of a shark, she would seemingly return my adoring gaze, then open her jaws, revealing deceptively tiny teeth, and clamp down on my nose (or my shoulder, in a popular variation) with the full force of her two-year-old strength. The pain was excruciating. Part of it was psychic—the indignity of a two-year-old biting you is real—but the physical pain was also severe. With stars shooting before my eyes, I resisted the impulse to inflict the same sort of pain in return. I wanted nothing more than to stoop to her level and bite back. Instead, I managed to form my mouth around the words, "DON'T BITE," which I released in a controlled scream. I tried not to give her the upper hand by showing her just how much her bite had hurt. And I didn't dwell on her aggressive behavior. I simply rebuked her sternly and left the room, giving myself some time away from her. Then we moved on.

Love Bites

Or at least I tried to. Biting strikes fear in the hearts of parents. A cute cuddly toddler masticating human flesh is incongruous, at the very least. And it is humiliating for the parents, who are made to feel they are somehow incapable of raising a civilized human being. Toddling biters are at risk of being kicked out of daycare; ostracized by friends; bitten in return.

It was apprehension about all of those possibilities that sent me scurrying to our bookshelves and to the on-line experts in search of an answer. I learned there are various theories on the origins of munchkin munching. It may be a form of expression for those still too young to communicate effectively in words, an interesting early study in cause and effect, a manifestation of control, a desire for more human contact, a cry of frustration, or simply an attempt to relieve teething gums.

Whatever the cause, Caroline reserved her bites for her father and me—except once. Expressing herself in the most powerful way she knew how, she turned her piranha-like jaws on her friend Luke. It was a defensive maneuver, a means of maintaining her position as driver of her Little Tikes car. The bite was a bad one. Luke was bruised for days. His mother, a true friend, called me a few days later to tell me she had spoken to her parents the day of the attack. They had laughed and informed her it was sweet revenge. Apparently, her own childhood biting was the stuff of legend. One woman's confession is another's absolution. The horrified guilt I'd been harboring hastily retreated upon hearing her words.

Luke was the last person Caroline bit. With my shame dissipated, her biting no longer filled my heart with trepidation and she seemed

179

to understand innately that she'd lost her power. After a nearly year-long struggle, the behavior ebbed as quietly and inexplicably as it had first flowed.

The epiphany came later, during a wrestling match between my husband and Caroline. She yelled out the two words in a low guttural voice; her intonation revealed everything. Anger, frustration, and annoyance had taken residence in those two small words, uttered in perfect mimicry of her mother's muddled attempts to thwart an exasperating behavior. She'd understood our displeasure all along, even if we couldn't understand the motivation behind her attacks. "Toe-bye." DON'T BITE. Suddenly, it all made sense.

Now, as her little five-year-old face presses close to mine, her cherubic mouth bestows only kisses—sweet elixir for this mother's soul.

Sunday Bloody Sunday

Annie Spiegelman

YAY, IT'S SUNDAY MORNING. Sun is shining. Morning is bright. I've got the day off! Read the *New York Times* in bed. Look into Bill's sleepy eyes and smirk. We can have a romantic breakfast in bed.

Oh wait . . . I forgot.

We have a two-year-old son named Jack who is best described as a perpetual motion machine. We are his parents. More meaningfully, we are "his people." We are on call 24/7. We are shamelessly unqualified for the job. We took on a lifetime commitment for a brief moment of pleasure. I think I'll close my eyes and just go back to sleep.

"WHAAAAAAAA-WHAAAA!"

I guess not. Crawl out of bed. Time to clock in. I'm back on duty. Somebody's got to negotiate us a better contract. Maybe I'll start a parenting union in my spare time.

Oh, wait . . . I don't have any spare time.

I don't have any kind of time.

Here come those fat little delicious feet stomping and thumping along the hardwood floors to our bedroom. My arms are open. My heart is smiling. Yet, all I really want to do is crawl back beneath the blankets and daydream. Me, alone, lying on a tropical beach. No one ever warned me motherhood would make me a master of wishing for two entirely contradictory things, alternating every other minute, and then feeling guilt-ridden and exhausted during the nanoseconds in between.

It is a beautiful sunny day in April. Bill suggests the three of us drive to Point Reyes for a mountain bike ride and a kayak trip. I married not only an exceptional athlete but a die-hard wilderness man too. We live in beautiful northern California, but deep inside I am still an escaped Type A New Yorker who grew up thinking Manhattan was the Center of the Universe and Central Park was the backwoods.

We pack up the Jeep. Jack grabs his militia of stuffed bunnies off the bed and fills the backseat with his entourage. Bill loads the inflatable kayak we borrowed from our friend Betty. I mount the bikes on the bike rack. I keep telling myself we are going to have a fun day, but deep down inside I know it's there. Patiently lurking. Waiting. Stalking. Disguised beneath that sweet, cherubic face lies all the necessary kindling for the mother of all tantrums.

We keep feeding Jack snacks so he doesn't get bored during the hourlong drive. He is not keen about sitting still for any length of time. Two soy milks and one Pop-Tart later, we arrive at the mountain bike trail without much fuss. I put Jack on the bike seat mounted behind me and we take off down the road. Bill and I are laughing as he details ad nauseam the different trees we bike past. Just to torture me. He knows all trees look the same to me and that I am absolutely certain there is some crazy person hiding behind each one.

Sunday Bloody Sunday

Just when I am beginning to think that maybe we *can* do fun family activities together, Jack begins crying. He dropped his sippy cup somewhere along the trail. We reluctantly turn around and spend the next twenty minutes searching for his cup with Jack hysterically crying in the most beautiful, serene country you could ever imagine. Two twenty-something cyclists speed by. They are surely wondering why we can't do something about that crying kid! The sippy cup is lost forever. We decide to end our bike ride.

In the car, we feed Jack crackers and cheese to keep his mind off the lost cup and the twenty-minute windy drive to Tomales Bay, where we intend to go kayaking. The food placates him for a while. We make it to the bay singing, *"Dang me, dang me. Ought to take a rope and hang me. Hang me from the highest tree"* over and over and over. Everyone is doing just fine when we arrive at the parking lot.

Except for two not-so-minor problems.

After manually inflating three-quarters of the kayak, we realize one of the screw caps to seal the air chamber is missing. Without it we cannot keep the kayak inflated. We search the car without success. Meanwhile, outside the car, Jack is behaving like a lunatic, running around the parking lot, growling, swatting bugs and birds with a kayak oar and shouting, "CHARGE!!" We let him go. We're too angry about the kayak. Who cares what others think of our child? Maybe we *are* lousy parents. All we want to do is grumble over how we got jilted and shortchanged on our bike ride and now our kayaking trip is going up in smoke too. Instead of grabbing the oar out of Jack's hands, we hastily load the kayak, all the while scheming up a good story to tell Betty about losing the screw cap or, better yet, a way to blame her for losing the cap and then suspiciously loaning us dangerous and faulty equipment. *"We could have drowned!"* I will tell her.

Once we're all packed and ready to go, the second not-so-minor problem occurs. I pick up Jack to put him in his car seat and he pukes all over me. Then he cries because he doesn't want to get in the car and have to endure the tortuously curvy back roads home. We decide to drive to a nearby nursery to clean up in their rest room. In the dusty cracked bathroom mirror I see one of those haggard, stressed-out moms I swore I'd never become. Outside it is a magnificent, warm Sunday afternoon and tranquil, hopeful gardeners are peacefully planning their spring perennial beds.

I stop to take in the serenity. Then I turn and notice Bill wandering around the nursery looking very, very miserable. I turn again and see Jack on the other side of the property nonchalantly skipping, pulling the name tags out of plants and throwing them up in the air while singing, "Yippeeee." I turn again and see two traumatized nurserymen pointing at Jack. I yell over to Bill. He runs toward Jack. I take a shortcut by leaping over boxwoods, lavenders, and, ouch, miniature rose bushes. I seize the perpetrator and hurry back to the parking lot with a blond moptop whirling dervish grabbing leaves off of plants, screaming and kicking wildly in the air.

"No, NO, NOOO! MAMA. NO, MAMA. You are the Mean Mama. HELP, HELP! HELP! LET ME GO! WHAAAAAAA! WHAAAAAA! WHAAAAA!"

I am out of breath, sweating, dizzy from hyperventilating. Sun block is dripping into my eyes. The acrid stench of soy-milk vomit saturates the air. I make it to the Jeep. People are staring at me as I strap my hysterical child into his car seat and emphatically slam the door. I snatch my sunglasses off and give them the evil eye.

Don't &@%# with me.

Bill slithers into the driver's seat, pretending he doesn't know us.

He tries to avert the onlookers' stares. We are not speaking. Jack's wailing soon subsides into quieter sobbing and sniffling. Nestled amongst his stuffed bunnies, teetering on the cusp of sleep, he laments, "Papa, this is the worstest day of my life."

We arrive home. Frustrated. Confused. But we are still standing, and our boy is asleep for the night. I tuck him into bed and kiss his soft cheeks. We unload the bikes and the busted kayak. It's been a long day. Bill heads for Jack's room while I put on a pot of tea. He returns, having heisted Jack's heart-shaped basket of chocolate Easter eggs (a gift from Grandma). Together the two of us sit back, relax, and enjoy a colorful sunset from our kitchen table, devouring every last delectable chocolate egg.

We are learning to appreciate the small things in life.

Queen of the World

Leanna James

THIS IS A STORY ABOUT AN ORDINARY AFTERNOON with my three-year-old daughter, Amanda, an afternoon that started with blocks and Play-Doh and ended with a mystery I have yet to solve.

The elements of this story are as familiar as porridge: a little friend, a pile of toys snatched from the toy box, another pile of dress-up gowns in pink and gold, a couple of plastic crowns. There are snacks of crackers, fruit, and juice. There is a toy flute I pretend to play as the girls dance. There is a game of hide-and-go-seek, another game of catch-the-kitty! stopped mid-chase, much to my daughter's disappointment (she loves crushing the cat to her body in a passionate toddler embrace). A short break for tears—"I wanted to hug kiiiityyy"—then a game called *nice*-not-*evil*-queen-in-the-castle, with much putting on and taking off of jewels, crowns, and gowns.

Then comes the play money. My daughter's playmate, Emma, parades around the house waving the money at various objects— "I'll take that, and that, and that." She buys an old vase stuffed with paper flowers, a beat-up pillow, an alligator puppet, a pair of red glitter shoes. Amanda giggles. "Store! We're playing store!"

I resist the urge to lecture my three-year-old on the evils of consumerism. Advertising, mass media, marketing to kids—my mind takes off like a speeding car, hot on the trail of Disney and Mattel. Amanda shouts: "I have a hundred dollars for the store. No, a million. My money goes all the way to the moon!"

But Emma isn't playing "store." Perhaps inspired by the impressive ladder of purple, yellow, and blue dollar bills, she announces a better plan: "No, Amanda, we're playing Queen of the World. I'm Queen and I can buy everything. I can buy all the people! I'm going to buy everyone in the world! Then all the people will belong to me!"

Amanda turns to me, her eyes suddenly wet, her face a tight mask of dismay. She opens and closes her mouth in the classic pantomime of shock, standing motionless on the rug, play money still clenched in her fist. Then her hand opens, the bills scatter to the floor, and Amanda lets out a howl so piercing that the cat, scrabbling in terror, dives under the couch.

"No! She can't buy people! Mommy, tell her! You can't own somebody, you can't, you can't! That's wrong! That's evil! Tell her, Mommy! No, Emma! I won't let you, I won't let you buy the people! Bad Emma! You stop it stop it stop it!"

Amanda, sobbing now, rushes at her friend and tries to wrestle the money away. Emma laughs at her—"What's the matter, you silly?"—as I swoop over and spirit Amanda to the other side of the room. We plop down on a pillow as Emma, baffled, shrugs and begins separating her money into different-colored stacks.

"Honey, it's okay, it's okay. She didn't mean any harm. It was just a game." I try to put my arms around Amanda, wipe the tears and a glisten of snot from her hot cheek.

"No." Amanda's shoulders tense; her hand flies out and bats mine away. Then she turns an accusing glance at me and repeats her objection, since I clearly haven't understood: "You can't buy *people,* Mommy!" Her voice is shaking, not with fear but with fire, her eyes shooting sparks that, for a moment, seem almost to burn my face.

"No, of course you can't buy people. You're right, sweetie. You're right."

She is not comforted, but eventually allows herself to be coaxed into doing a puzzle, the handmade wooden pieces forming a jolly train that snakes into the kitchen. "All aboard to Popsicle Land!" I announce as I head for the freezer, shamelessly pulling the oldest one of all from Mommy's Bag of Tricks.

Later, with Emma gone and the play money discreetly thrown away with the Popsicle sticks, I began sorting through the pieces of my own puzzle: What was that about? Where on earth did that come from, how did she "know"? I hadn't told her that, in fact, her great-great grandparents had been "owned." When, exactly, is the right time to share that information? To tell your child that some of her ancestors were brought to this country in chains? It's not the first choice that comes to mind for a bedtime story, not the sort of tale that ends with a castle and a feast and villagers dancing around a glittering, vanquished dragon. The kind of story in which the world is just. The kind I wish were always true.

But Amanda doesn't live in a pastel storybook village. She knows that people come in lots of colors. She shared this discovery with me one morning on the way home from preschool, chatting happily in her car seat: "Mommy, know what? Some of my friends are brown, like Daddy, and some are peach like me, and some are pink like you!" Pretty accurate description—but it hadn't gone much further than that yet. Martin Luther King, Jr., Day was observed with a day off from school ("No Blue Room today, honey"), not with speeches and banners and curriculum units, all of which would come later. Her father and I were preparing; having long talks at night, studying books, rehearsing answers for the questions she would someday ask.

But not this soon. We didn't think she was ready for a truth so stark and ugly, didn't believe it was right to burden her at this age with a history so at odds with her harmonious, multicultural world. Yet the burden had shown up on its own, a weighty package on our doorstep.

When her father came home that night, I told him the story and we dutifully brought it up as we were tucking Amanda into bed. "What bothered you about the 'buying people' game, sweetheart? Did you hear something at school? Did someone say something to you about being black?"

Amanda looked at us, bewildered. "Why would they say that?"

"Well, because . . ." her father began.

"Why, Daddy?" Amanda sat up, knocking her stuffed tiger to the floor.

Here we go. Earnest, measured, using the carefully soothing tones of a pediatric nurse about to give a shot, we introduced the "s" word: "Umm, do you know what a slave is, darling?"

She blinked confusedly, then lit up. "Like when Cinderella has to do all the work?"

"Ahh. Sort of, yes, right idea. But . . ." Deep breath. "Do you know what happened to black people a long time ago?"

"Why were they black a long time ago?"

"No, no," her father said, as we both struggled between laughter and alarm. "I mean, yes, they were, but people are black now, too." He pointed to himself. "Like me, honey."

"Oh, Daddy, you're not black," Amanda said helpfully. "You're *brown*."

"Well, yes, but *black* means—okay, remember about that country called Africa? Where Daddy's ancestors came from a long time ago?"

Africa! Yes, yes, she knew all about Africa; there were lions and elephants—Babar was one.

And so it went, until she got annoyed and told us she was tired and asked us to read *Babar*. She fell asleep during the wedding scene, as Babar was dancing under the stars with his elephant bride, lions and rhinos stomping joyfully around them.

Her father and I went to bed. We wondered, as we wonder still, what force in her was present that day, what knowledge or memory turned her play from a lighthearted game to a moral showdown. Something we'd said in passing, a fragment of conversation overheard from her crib? Or perhaps something remembered from before her time, from a line of distant people whose atoms live on in the tissues and muscles and veins of her small body. "It's in the blood." You hear grandmothers saying things like this. "She was born with it." Born with what, I want to know. Born with a memory of people being bought and sold? Or had she been the one sold, the spirit I know as "Amanda" present in another body, another time?

Maybe someday I will know. Until then, I watch as my daughter cries out against playground injustice, spit flying from the gap between her front teeth. She stands up for the kid being teased, throws sand at a classmate found poking a spider with a stick ("He was poking too hard. The spider didn't like it!"). She knows, in some core part of her, what it is to suffer—and to make another suffer. If she had her way, power and pain would be banished from the earth—or at least from her tiny patch of it. "Don't boss your servants around!" Amanda scolds a bad-tempered queen in one of her picture books. Later, I find she's taken her children's scissors and cut the queen right out of the pages. Some of the illustrations have been changed, too. In the servants' cottage, atop a rough wooden table, a steaming pot drawn in firm brown crayon has mysteriously appeared. "Bean soup," Amanda explains. "Will you draw a cake, Mama? They want dessert, too."

With a pink crayon, I make a three-layer cake and top it with strawberries. Her father comes in, grabs the crayons and adds a big jug of milk. Then, as an afterthought, he flips to the last page of the book, turns it over, and on the blank side carefully draws a horse and wagon.

"Who's that, Daddy?" Amanda asks, enchanted with the horse. "Is he in the story?"

"He is now," her father smiles.

"But what's the wagon for?"

"For the servants, of course. To ride away in."

"Oh! *Yes!*" Amanda gives the scullery maid, the stable boy, and the washerwoman each a bag of gold—"I *need* a glitter crayon, Mommy"—and off they go, pockets full of gold pieces and cake, into the future my daughter creates for them.

Playing with Potatoes

Putnam Goodwin-Boyd

IT's SEVEN O'CLOCK. My wife has just showered our son with hugs, kisses, and good-byes. As she heads off, Samuel toddles to our glass front door and gazes at her until she disappears into the car. He is a big toddler, and people often guess he is much older than he is. He learned to walk early because hauling his heavy, solid body around in a crawl was too much work. Still, as he stands at the door, gently tapping the glass, his oversized bald head fixated on his mom, uttering a short combination of sounds and baby words, you can really tell he's just a year old. Momma pulls out. Sam turns away, gazing around the living room, deciding where to begin the morning. I'm not going to be very entertaining. Sam was up three times in the night and even though it doesn't seem to be affecting him, the best I can do is sit on the couch, watch him, and wait for the caffeine to kick in.

Sam is our first, and one of only a few of his generation in our large extended family. He has received toys from every relative and friend we have ever known. He owns mountains of toys: eye-catching, brightly colored, shiny abstract shapes and soft and squishy animals that emit noises when squeezed or stepped upon. Our home is like a toy warehouse, and Sam spends many of his waking hours roaming from spot to spot, applying short, intense bursts of energy to one object and then moving on to the next.

This morning, he begins near the door, babbling to a stuffed alien he dropped there earlier. He sticks the alien's tail in his mouth and swings the creature from side to side. After a while a toy truck catches his eye. The alien drops to the floor as Sam staggers over, plops down next to the truck, and begins to pat it. Soon he's on to something else, a concerned expression on his face as he rambles about looking for fun. His eyebrows furrow and his lips purse. This is his job. The gaze and touch he applies to each object seems to probe not only its surface quality, but its inner essence. He seeks to unlock the toyness in everything he encounters, not just the things we adults call toys, but everything. All morning long he is on a mission to be amused.

As I watch, bleary-eyed, from the couch, stirring only to refill my coffee cup or move dangerous and breakable things from Sam's reach, I begin to notice a pattern, or perhaps a lack of pattern, in the things Sam chooses. None of the commercially produced "toys" capture Sam's attention any more than the everyday objects he encounters in his travels.

When Sam was six months old, we took out some plastic linking blocks we thought he might enjoy. He never was interested in the blocks, but he was quite taken by the lid of the plastic container they came in. He smacked it on the ground, drummed it, chewed it, threw it across the room, and chased after it. Seeing Sam play with the container top inspired me to try a plastic coffee-can lid on him. He was instantly delighted. He chewed, threw, and hammered the lid for several minutes. Now, yogurt, coffee-can, and cottage-cheese container lids are spread all around the house. I can almost always count on a lid to hold his attention when all other things fail.

A cylindrical oatmeal container is minding its own business in the middle of the living room rug. Sam approaches it exuberantly, pounces on it, then scuttles after it as it rolls away. Our house is old and the floors are tilted, so once the oatmeal container begins to roll, it can go for quite a while. Sam retrieves it and starts to use it as a bongo drum. His stumpy fingers are spread wide and they make a dry slapping sound at first. Then he accidentally hits the right spot with his palm and gets an unexpected resonant thump. He grins, coos, and drools with pleasure. He pounces again, this time squeezing the top off the container. He gazes into the can's inner depths, then tries to get his mouth into the hole. Finally, he makes a noise and discovers he has an echo chamber in his hands. I can't see his mouth, but I can tell by his eyes he is grinning again.

A cardboard case of diapers lies near the couch. I use it as a footrest. Sam now moves toward it, determined to practice his climbing. When he first learned to pull himself upright on the couch, he did it over and over, pulling up, then flopping back down suddenly on his diapered bottom. I know the routine, and I know I had better move the diaper box to the center of the living room and put it on top of a comforter. I also have to shift from the couch to the floor, get in a position to catch Sam if he falls.

The box serves as a primitive jungle gym. Sam pulls himself upright, climbs on top, then hops back down. He looks at me and waits. I've forgotten: I'm supposed to sing "Tadaaa!" when he lands.

When I finally say it, he repeats his stunt, over and over and over. At first he is cautious, hesitating before jumping, his body tense as he lands. One-year-olds seem to be unsure about the general principles of gravity. Eventually, Sam grows to trust that the floor will always be there, not giving way when he lands. His shoulders relax, and he squeals after each landing. I call this activity baby step aerobics.

After all that exercise, Sam sits and starts putting things in his mouth. Now I have to be extra-vigilant, because Sam's major baby liability is the extra-large mouth he has inherited from his father. He can and will fit things in his mouth that the average baby hippo would have difficulty with. He'll pop virtually anything in there. It's best not to have anything smaller than his head within reach, particularly right before mealtime.

The mail arrives. As I sort through the pile, it occurs to me that the junk mail might satisfy Sam's shredding desires. Sam has a strong urge to destroy anything made of paper or cardboard. Judging by the look on his face, there is something deeply primal going on when he shreds. He systematically turns any magazine that crosses his path into a pile of confetti. The last step of this process is to eat the pieces of paper he has shredded. I hand him the junk mail and watch with extreme satisfaction as all those unsolicited credit card offers are mangled beyond recognition.

My main role in a morning of play is to distract Sam from all things dangerous and fragile by waving more benign offerings in front of him and putting the problematic objects out of reach, a task which is growing more difficult as he becomes more mobile. I'm Sam's personal OSHA representative. I must admit, on days like this, it is challenging to assess all the dangerous things a one-year-old can do with, say, an adult sneaker. If it amuses him, I'm inclined to let him play away. Only when he has licked the sole or whacked himself on the head with it do I reconsider.

Sam toddles behind the island in the kitchen. This is definitely a place where he has to be monitored. Most truly dangerous things are out of reach, but he can make a mess of the low, cluttered shelves within seconds. I peek around the corner to discover that he has found what he has really wanted all morning: a potato.

There is something about the heft of a mid-sized baker that really intrigues him. The minute he comes in contact with one he beams. He loves the sound it makes as he rolls it on the floor. As soon as it comes to rest he scuttles after it, not wanting to be parted from it for long. Then he picks it up and puts it down again and again and again. When he's in a more pensive frame of mind, Sam will just hold his potato, gazing upon its surface as if it were a crystal ball revealing to him the secrets of the universe. Pound for pound, at this point in his life, no other toy provides as much entertainment potential as a potato.

My wife works nearby, and comes home for lunch every day. As she eats, then snuggles and plays with Sam, I review for her the events of the morning. It has been a simple, yet pleasurable one. There will come a day when Sam loses interest in all these mundane things. I know I used to take them for granted before he came along. Meanwhile, he teaches us that life is so much richer when lids are for throwing, boxes for climbing upon, and potatoes for more than just eating.

Fix Me

Elisabeth Rose Gruner

NICK SITS IN THE BATH, singing in his warbly baby voice. "Oh—
oh, fix me. Oh—oh, fix me. Oh—oh, fix me, fix me, Jesus, fix me."
His off-key rendition bounces off the tile walls. Where did he learn
this song? We sang it recently in church, I guess; I didn't know he
was paying attention.

I'm not a theologian, but the hymn "Fix me, Jesus" has always
troubled me. First of all, there's the refrain: "fix me." We start out
with the notion that we're broken. I can accept that I am, but Nick
is two-and-a-half, just a baby. His large brown eyes fix me in their
liquid gaze. His curls fall around his face, framing his babyish smile.
He's not broken. I struggle with the concept of original sin.

The song goes on to speak of "my long white robe" and "my journey
home." My choir director, Martha, says to remember that spirituals were
sung in slavery times and that death was sometimes the only freedom,
the only home, that the slave could know. Even so, my son is not a slave.
And I don't like to think of his "journey home"—not yet, not ever.

I take Nick to church because it's where I go on Sunday mornings
and I want him to be with me. I take Nick to church because I was

taken there every Sunday morning during my childhood. At some deep level church means home to me and I want it to mean home to him. I take Nick to church because I love him. But "Fix me, Jesus"? This hymn and others like it remind me that I'm not in my father's church, where emotion is reined in and spirituality is not really discussed. My father, an Episcopal priest, tends to speak of alienation rather than sin, selects hymns of praise rather than contrition. This church I've chosen is freer with emotion, more open to the personal experience of brokenness and suffering that brings so many people to church these days. It's open, as well, to the children who roam the aisles during the service, who, like Nick, often sing and speak out of turn, amusing and annoying their neighbors. I like it, I think, but sometimes the differences bring me up short.

John the Evangelist says, "In the beginning was the Word," and for me, faith has always begun in the words, the religious language that has surrounded me since I was born. The language of the church suffuses me, inspires me, even angers me; I am woven into its fabric and it into mine. It echoes in my brain as I drive, as I walk, as I read and think and dream. Sometimes when I apologize, I think to myself, *We have erred and strayed from thy ways like lost sheep.* Before communion, I hear a prayer, no longer common, echoing within: *"We do not presume to come to this thy table, O Lord, trusting in our own righteousness . . . We are not worthy so much as to gather up the crumbs under thy table . . ."* Many of these words and phrases, I see as I type them, have to do with unworthiness, with failure, with loss. "Fix me," indeed. I've been saying it all my life.

• • •

Nick kisses the statue of the boy Jesus in the Lady Chapel. Nick calls him "Big Boy Jesus" to distinguish him from the Baby Jesus in the painting over the altar. It's a carved wooden statue of a mother and son. Her hand is on his shoulder but he's standing on his own, not quite ready to walk away, but moving in that direction. Next year, or the year after, Big Boy Jesus will take off, walk away from Mary and not check back. He's about Nick's height. I like the Lady Chapel; it speaks to me as both a mother and a child. I'm glad Nick likes it, too.

Like Big Boy Jesus, Nick's not walking away from me yet. He wants me with him in the bathroom, as he rides his bike outside, as he eats and watches TV and plays. Just my presence—the hand on his shoulder—is enough. Like the boy Jesus, he will walk away one day. I'll be left standing behind, wondering where he's gone.

We walk out of the Lady Chapel and Nick says, "When I grow up I want to be a Big Boy Jesus." Pause. "And a speed racer."

"Okay," I say, "you see if you can."

I'm not quite sure what either of us means.

Some months later we're at communion on Maundy Thursday, the commemoration of the Last Supper. The congregants are gathered around the altar, a square table of marble and wood. The priest holds up the rough round loaf of brown bread. She says, "On the night he was handed over to suffering and death, our Lord Jesus Christ took bread; and when he had given thanks to you, he broke it, and gave it to his disciples, and said, 'Take, eat: This is my Body, which is given for you. Do this for the remembrance of me.'"

Fix Me

Nick, still a literalist, stage-whispers to me, "That's not Jesus' body." He's not developmentally ready for the metaphoric thinking that allows me to accept the bread as body. On another level, of course, metaphor is all he has, lacking the experience to fix language as firmly as adults do (or try to). The shifts he makes, the "mistakes," teach me anew how arbitrary our language is, and how necessary. Recently he walked away from communion grimacing. "Mommy, I need some water to get that salvation out of my mouth," he said.

We're taught that God gave Adam the power to name. In naming, in saying "this bread is the body of Christ," we make meaning, we "fix" a relationship, forge it for our use. We are part of the divine, then, as we make language, as we make sense and even nonsense out of the stuff of grocery lists and phone books, novels and verse.

When I became an English professor I returned to the origins of my faith, to language and its various abilities and disabilities. I am confronted with them again in my son, whose understanding and language are still so unformed, so full of potential.

Going to church feeds my imagination, as it does Nick's. He wants to come to church with me, tries to sing the songs, talks about Jesus. One day he tells me he is mad at Jesus because the people wanted him to be a super king. "Do you want him to be a super king?" I ask. "No," Nick replies, "I want you to be a super king." The power he wants to invest in me both scares and delights me. Later he returns to the story: "The people were mad at Jesus so they chased him but he was up there," he points skyward. "But then they came and shooted him and he was dead."

I think "killed" equals "shooted" in his mind, and why shouldn't it? Do we really have to talk about nails and crosses? Aren't guns bad enough? Isn't it bad enough that he already knows—sort of—what killing is, and that guns are involved, and yet wants to play with them every day?

Real guns and real killings are all too common in this city. One day after preschool he looked up at me and asked, "Mommy, do you know what guns are for?" His eyes widened as he waited for my response.

"No, Nick, tell me, what are guns for?"

"They're for Bidden," he answered.

I can see it now, a preschool full of children sitting around waiting for Bidden to come and get the guns, waiting for Godot, waiting for the second coming, waiting. In the meantime they roll up the pictures they've painted and "shoot" each other with them. Is this part of what we mean when we sing "Fix me"? That humans are so alienated that we love violence, that we turn it into play? I resist the notion, preferring to think that Nick and his friends don't understand what they're doing. Their metaphoric guns are not really guns, just rolled-up paper, just pointed fingers.

I tell Martha about Nick's singing "Fix me, Jesus." She is touched and pleased, and the next time she sees Nick she gathers a group around him to serenade him. We work the harmonies, emphasizing

Fix Me

the near-dissonance that suddenly resolves. I love gospel harmonies, even when the words stick in my throat. Nick doesn't sing along. When I buckle him into his car seat afterward, I ask him about the song. Did he like it? "Yes, fix me, Cheesis," he seems to say.

"What, Nick?" I ask.

"Fix me Cheez-Its," he answers clearly. "Can we get some Cheez-Its for lunch?"

Possession

Meredith Small

"I NEED SOME GLUE."

These are words that strike terror into the heart of any mother with a three-year-old.

"What do you need glue for?" I asked my daughter, dreading the answer. Sure enough, clutched in her tiny fist were two of my very lovely, very expensive, silk scarves.

"I want to glue these together," she said, waving her next art project in my face.

"You can't do that," I responded, with all the grown-up authority I could muster. "They are *mine*, not *yours*."

And thus begins, for the three hundredth time that day, yet another lesson in who owns what.

The scarves are mine. The dolly is yours. The book is Daddy's. The desk is mine. The pen is Daddy's. The crayon is yours.

By the end of the day, I have earmarked every item in the house as belonging to someone, and have explained over and over that she is only allowed to touch what is hers.

My daughter, of course, has no trouble understanding the ideas of "mine" and "yours." Human children, linguists tell us, are hard-wired to acquire words and meanings. They know, easy as pie, what it means to take possession, to own something.

Our chat is not a language lesson, it's a social one. The point is to make her understand, as a good citizen, that people own things and other people don't get to take them.

As a parent, I'd like to believe that all parents, everywhere, are going through this same ritual. But as an anthropologist, I know that this is simply not true. There are many places where possessing something is not an issue.

In nomadic cultures, for example, people are always on the move and they can't carry all that much. The camel is Dad's, the cooking pot is Mom's, and that's all there is—the list is short.

Hunters and gatherers have so little that they are apt to share what they have, even with children. The digging stick is Mom's but her child can try it out. The machete is Dad's but anyone can use it to clear a path.

And there are cultures, such as the Mbuti Pygmies of Central Africa's Ituri forest, in which there is no possession at all because everything belongs to everybody.

The pygmies believe that sharing and connection are the most important values in life. They act as a collective, passing goods, daily chores, and even children around. Everyone is responsible, everyone shares. No pygmy mother would ever point to anything and say "it's mine" because she owns nothing and everything.

But in our world, we believe in the individual, the person who owns things privately. And so I spend my day inducting my daughter into our culture, drawing and redrawing the lines of ownership.

And sometimes, I know the lessons have hit home, only too well.
"Can Mommy have a bite of your cookie, sweetheart?"
"No, it's mine. All mine. Not yours."
Oh, how I wish we were pygmies.

The Rules

Jennifer Niesslein

CALEB AND I ARE IN LINE at the grocery store one blustery afternoon before a storm. He's in the back of the cart, examining a new
box of Scooby-Doo Band-Aids. Ahead of us in line is an older
couple. The woman turns around and her eyes light up when she
spots Caleb, my handsome boy, all big brown eyes and spaghetti
sauce-flecked shirt. "Do you know what you have?" she says to him.
Oh crap, I think. *It's coming*. "Pink cheeks," she says. She moves in
to touch his cheek. And, of course, it happens.

Down goes the Scooby-Doo box. He tries to smack her hand
away, narrowly missing. "Leave me alone!" he hollers.

Caleb's three. I'm speechless. On the one hand, I know that the
woman was only trying to be nice; I also understand that someday
I will be in my sixties, and a touch of those flushed toddler cheeks
will be a precious commodity. On the other hand, I don't like
strangers touching me, either. And I'm happy that Caleb forces
people to respect his personal space. In the end, I busy myself in the
wilderness that is my purse. I don't correct Caleb. I don't apologize
for him, either. I give the woman a quick smile.

I don't know what that smile was supposed to mean. But I do know that it's quite possible she turned away thinking, *Brat.* It's something I think about a lot. One of my biggest fears is that I am raising a brat, a child who thinks the rules don't apply to him.

I don't think Caleb is a brat. But I look at how we run things around here and have to acknowledge the potential is there. He's at the age when every decision can escalate into a full-on, scream-loud-enough-for-the-neighbors-to-hear battle—so we choose our battles carefully. We pick the ones that we'll win. As a result, the rules at our house are few. Want mac and cheese for breakfast? Sure! Feel like watching TV for a couple of hours? Hey, why not? Can only get to sleep snuggled down in Mama's and Daddy's bed? Pile on, kiddo.

The problem is that the difference between a brat and a kid who can see the world as flexible is just a line in the sand. My husband and I are the ones drawing that line for Caleb, and nobody really knows if it's in the right place. Are there too few rules? Not the right ones? Will Caleb, lacking lots of rules at home, disregard rules in the larger world? Years down the road, will we have a confident, spontaneous son who has the skills to always land on his feet? Or will we have a little Sid Vicious on our hands, spitting in restaurants and yelling curse words at the elderly?

That I'm a rule follower from way back only intensifies the issue. I cannot imagine failing to RSVP or cutting in line. When, after several days of the latest family flu, I realized we were a day late in paying my son's preschool tuition, I panicked. "We're late on the tuition!" I moaned several times to my husband as the miserable three of us lolled around in our wrinkled pajamas. Perhaps sensing that I was gunning for him to drive the check to the school, my husband responded with only a sleepy, "Yes, we are." I padded into the kitchen to look at the clock; by the time I reached the school, it would be closed anyway. With a sinking feeling, I acknowledged that we would be The Flaky Parents Who Create Unnecessary Work for the Nice Preschool Staff. In my fevered sleep that night, I dreamt of the preschool's assistant director, tapping glumly on her computer, unable to meet payroll, all for lack of our $79.50 by Wednesday at five. I know it sounds ridiculous. But rules exist for a reason, and if I'm going to be someone's pain in the ass, I want it be for something that matters.

The other day, Caleb and I were playing Candy Land, a game of few but firm rules. We were taking turns. We were picking cards from the top of the deck. We were having a grand old rule-following time.

Then, he pointed at Rainbow Trail, a space a few squares from where his gingerbread man was. "I want to go here."

"Well, honeybun," I said. "If you pick an orange card next, you can."

He drew from the deck. It was Queen Frostine, a card that would whisk him away from my piece and put him much closer to winning. But, no.

"I don't want this card!" he told me. "I want to go to Rainbow Trail!" He wriggled on the floor, and his voice became dismayed and rather shocked, as if accepting the Queen Frostine card would send him on a tour of the local septic plant. I told him that if he couldn't play by the rules, then maybe we should stop playing. I pointed out that the Queen Frostine card was *good,* that if he put his guy up there, he could get closer to the castle. No dice. We stopped playing. I picked up a magazine. He took his gingerbread man and slid it along Rainbow Trail, up and down, up and down.

I'd be hard put to say that that was bratty behavior. Some people would call it age-appropriate; they might even say that his reworking of Candy Land is a sign of his creativity, a subversive act that should be encouraged. But these people, unlike me, were not staring down an afternoon of what amounts to randomly scooting pieces of plastic around a sheet of cardboard. The thought of playing Anarchy in Candy Land made me boil with boredom.

It all worked out in this case. We both got a more appealing option: for me, a little uninterrupted reading, for him, doing just what he wanted. Caleb is a boy who knows what he wants. He decided that his grandmother should be called "Go-Go"; he's a child who will flop down on my lap and demand, "Tickle me everywhere" (but especially at the nape of his soft-skinned neck). Sometimes his desires conform to the rules, like when he insists that other kids at the playground play in a manner he deems safe (standing on the monkey bars is a big no-no, in his estimation). Sometimes his desires don't conform: he went through a cleaning phase in which everything he could reach—books, eyeglasses, the cordless phone—was tossed, with a flourish of his dimpled fist, into the "tash."

I don't have the cash to throw away cordless phones, but sometimes we do let Caleb learn for himself the consequences of bucking the rules. Eat too much candy and your belly hurts. Go to sleep too late and you're tired the next day. Tease the dog and eventually he won't want to play with you.

The rules I'm most concerned about are the ones where there aren't any real consequences. Ones that exist just to make life pleasant. We're big on manners, but social graces are much harder to teach. In the post office, a man smiles at Caleb. Caleb gives his dinosaur growl, one eyebrow cocked and his hands limp-wristed in Tyrannosaurus rex position. It's cute now but in five years it'll just be odd. My impulse is to tell him, "Be nice." Make that a rule.

But we don't live in a wholly nice world, and rules like these bring up some uncomfortable issues I have with the world we do live in. We have to, in many ways, conform to society to reap the benefits of living in it— yet I want him to make his voice heard when he confronts ugliness. I want to tell him to be nice to everyone he encounters but at the same time tell him to stick right with me because he's too little to fight off people who might hurt him. I'd like to advise him to respect his elders although he's already aware that age doesn't necessarily confer special wisdom. I want to tell him to simply get along with others, but I also want him to speak up when someone is offensive. I'm afraid blanket rules on interacting with the world will stunt the development of his own judgment. I won't always be there to tell him that calling someone a "grayhole"—Caleb's version of a swear word—isn't a good idea. I won't always be there to make the call: brat-like behavior or admirable speaking out?

For now, I leave the murky area alone, and so we're left with the few concrete rules we've erected at our house, plus that old chestnut, The Golden Rule. I imagine we'll make up a few more bylaws as he gets older. I hope they're enough to ward off brattiness. He's now encountering places where there are more rules than there are at home: Grandma and Grandpa's house, restaurants, preschool. It's a crazy world, I tell you. Grandma makes him take his shoes off indoors. In restaurants, he has to eat at the table.

At Caleb's preschool, I recently watched ten three-year-olds line up just as their teacher asked. They did the Hokey Pokey, putting their right hands in, mumbling along the words just under their teacher's alto. At the end, they clapped vigorously at their performance and went right to their cubbies to get cards for their parents. They were dressed as reindeer, complete with construction-paper antlers and cotton-ball tails. Nine of them had red, painted noses. Caleb had refused his stage makeup.

I accepted my card, kissed him, and loaded up his plate with sugary treats that, in a few hours, would cause him to behave in ways that make me want to swear at him. I marveled at how his teacher had gotten all ten kids to cooperate. . . . All those rules. And it seemed to me that Caleb understood that the rules do apply to him. Mostly.

An American Toddler
in Mexico

Morrey McElroy

BEFORE WE HAD CHILDREN, my husband and I lived for a while outside the small village of Fortín de las Flores in central Mexico. We taught English there at a small branch university nestled near the bottom of a coffee-covered hillside. Every weekend and holiday, we threw backpacks into our little red pickup truck and hit the road. By the end of the school year, our road atlas of Mexico was soft and worn, taped in several places. Colorful highlighting traced our routes over mountain ranges, across arid deserts, through lush tropical forests, and past ancient Olmec, Aztec, and Zapotec ruins. A year and a half later, living back home in New Orleans, we decided to return to Mexico for a summer road trip. This time we would be driving a green minivan with an eighteen-month-old baby boy strapped into the backseat. Our plans caused a furrowing of the collective family brow. Mexico, they said, had bad drinking water and road bandits. It was no place for a toddler. We disagreed and began stocking up on animal crackers, diapers, and Pedialyte. In early July, we headed south.

It wasn't long before we realized that romping through Mexico with a toddler was trickier than we had anticipated. Unexpected obstacles and danger zones popped up like moving targets in a carnival arcade. *"No, gracias,"* I would politely say to a kind-faced mother offering Henry a handful of large hard candies, her own children's cheeks bulging with the forbidden and hazardous treats. In Puebla, my husband's face blanched as Henry made a dash for a spiked iron fence low enough to impale him. Walking through a lively market, I steered Henry away from strings of red chili peppers and low open griddles popping with hot oil.

Mexico, it seemed, was not so different from the place imagined by our anxious families. And yet, toddlers were everywhere: dashing across rooftop terraces, climbing narrow winding staircases, and running down steep cobblestone walkways while their parents casually chatted nearby. In this apparent disorder, it was often difficult to discern which children belonged to which adults. My eyes would frantically search for the parent of an imperiled two-year-old as I mentally raced through the steps for child CPR and emergency first aid.

But, after a few tense days, I noticed something. When a child teetered on the edge of a fountain or reached toward a mangy dog, some adult would scoop him up, place him out of harm's way, and return calmly to the interrupted conversation. Once I realized the "neglected" children were in competent and caring hands, this relaxed style of parenting gradually began to seem sane. Certainly, it appeared less stressful than my own method. I decided to try it. With every step that Henry took away from me I began to accept the possibility of space between us. A vigilant eye was necessary. A death grip was not. I marveled at my son's small strong body as he marched ahead of me. Eventually, I almost enjoyed watching as Henry toddled up and down one set of stone steps after another.

Every town and village in Mexico has a central *zócalo*, or town square. These open public places, often flanked by stunning churrigueresque cathedrals and municipal palaces, are beautiful and functional. They serve as gathering places for businessmen having a quick smoke or a shoeshine, sanctuaries for teenage boys and girls sitting close together on shady benches, markets for vendors selling everything from cheap plastic pinwheels to exquisite handcrafted blankets and rugs, refuges for weary beggars. Children flock to the *zócalos* drawn by the constant swirl of motion and the high sweet whistle of the balloon man, his body so buried in colorful blown-up animals and polka dot balls that only his feet show. Henry was enchanted. He would twist his chubby little hand out of mine and run headlong into the bright Mexican sunlight. Instantly he was enveloped in a collage of color and activity.

In his mind, things in Mexico were as they should be. He was running, always running. In Saltillo he ran in circles around an ornate fountain, laughing as sprays of water formed little rainbows in the air. In Real de Catorce he ran with dust-covered street children playing hide-and-seek around a deteriorating bandstand. In Puebla, he made a game of running through a maze of several small square gardens. Now and then, he would stop in front of us, strike his toddler version of a muscleman pose, and then dash off again, his tiny fists pumping purposefully by his sides. In Tlaxcala, he ran through a plaza filled with clear airy bubbles. Along with a dozen twirling children he shrieked with delight as he darted to catch the glistening spheres. Chasing pigeons became a passion in the *zócalo* of San Luis Potosí. Spotting a flock sunning on the warm terracotta plaza, he ran to join them. A soft cloud of gray and iridescent purple burst into the air as he raised his face and arms toward the brilliant blue sky, his laughter joining the noisy chaos of beating wings. A local vendor was caught in the swirl of pigeons. Instead of shaking a fist at our son, he smiled toothlessly and watched as Henry headed off to join the birds for the hundredth time.

There were also moments of stillness and quiet observation. On a shady stone balcony, Henry carefully plucked fuchsia bougainvillea leaves from a gnarled vine and dropped them one by one until they formed a vibrant pink pool around his feet. Next to a lonely hilltop chapel, he bent to the ground and closely examined small fragments of worn colored tiles. With astonishing delicacy, he stroked each faded treasure before placing it in his pocket. Overwhelmed by an enormous wall mural in Tlaxcala, he reached up to my husband. Secure in his father's arms, Henry stared intently at the striking images of fierce Aztec warriors, sleek jaguar gods, and plumed serpents. His face tightened in concentration as he attempted to name what he saw. "Snake." "Cat." His eyes roamed the panoramic painting and settled on a wounded Indian—"bobo," he said softly.

One evening Henry stood on our hotel balcony overlooking the central *zócalo* in San Luis Potosí. From the darkened interior of the room, I could see his small body outlined by the late afternoon sun. We would be heading back to New Orleans soon, and I wondered what he would remember about this trip, what he would miss. The apple juice in his sippy cup had been replaced by more exotic fare—papaya, mango, and *guanábana*. He had danced under a full moon to the spirited tunes of a pan flute and mandolin, joining a parade of children too moved by the music to stay in their parents' laps. He had climbed ancient pyramids. What would he think, returning to the safely rounded play structure back home in Audubon Park?

Henry pressed his forehead to the iron rail of the balcony and watched the activity below. Young couples and families strolled by eating ice cream and sweet fried *churros*. Two young men with guitars sat cross-legged in the empty bandstand. They bent their heads in private laughter and occasionally plucked out *una canción de amor*. An elderly woman sat on a stone bench picking up loose red roses from the pile in her lap. She deftly gathered the flowers into bright bundles and dropped them one by one into a large basket at her feet.

As a golden light washed across the plaza, heavy cathedral bells began tolling the hour. Henry turned his head toward the deep melodic tones. It was a noise that had frightened him when we first arrived in Mexico, but now he stood still and listened intently, one small hand pointing toward the massive church. The dense ringing grew to a magnificent crescendo vibrating the air around us and marking the end of another day in this soulful country. As the last rich notes melted into the air a voice called up, *"¡Hola, guapo!"* (hello, handsome). *"¡Hola!"* Henry called back, *"¡Hola!"*

Potty Prattle

Kerri Peterson

As a physician, I find it easy to give advice. I spend a good part of my clinical practice counseling patients on diet, exercise, safe sex, seat-belting, and parenting skills. I listen to their frustration when their best efforts to heed my counsel yield minimal results. I smile and nod, suspecting that they are not following my advice. If they were, their cholesterol would be under two hundred; they would have lost that extra twenty pounds; their children would be better behaved. Yet when *my* problems refuse to yield to good common sense and self-discipline, I am resentful and confused. Such is the case with my four-year-old triplets, who are all *still* in diapers.

I have tried everything. I have faithfully followed the advice of all the best parenting books: I didn't start potty training too early, I didn't push, I didn't pressure, I didn't punish. I introduced them to the idea at the age of two, when they first came to me requesting diaper changes. That was what the experts recommended; that was the advice I'd given to numerous other mothers. At first, they seemed to enjoy sitting on the potty. They didn't *do* much while sitting there, but they made the effort painlessly.

Great, I thought. *This is going to be easy. My life of three-boys-in-diapers will soon be over!*

No such luck. Almost two years later, we still go through nearly a hundred diapers per week. I have devoured the toilet-training section of every parenting book at the local bookstore, hoping for some new modality, some heretofore unthought-of trick to get my boys interested. I've tried boasting, bargaining, bribing, beleaguering. I've tried star charts and toilet targets. I've bought every available design of kiddy toilet—in *triplicate!* I've tried taking the pressure off completely, hiding the potty chairs for months at a time, hoping the boys would eventually inquire as to their whereabouts. I've even tried letting them run around all day without diapers, hoping that their nakedness would remind them to run for the potty when their legs felt the first drip. "The Resistant Toddler," reads the chapter title of one book. I flip through these pages eagerly. I have, of course, already tried all its suggestions. At the end, I read the sentence which caps off the chapter on toilet-training resistance in every parenting manual: "If all else fails, consult your family physician."

I *am* a family physician.

I am also a single, working mother of three very different sons. They seem to have only one trait in common: their resistance to toilet training. A typical morning for us runs something like this: Ryker gets up first, having fallen asleep long before his brothers the night before. He is the most precocious of my sons; he knows his own mind, and speaks it. I take off his wet diaper and lead him to the potty as soon as he comes downstairs.

"There's no pee in my penis," Ryker explains. "I'll try after breakfast."

"*Everyone* has pee in their penis right after they wake up," I remind him. "Why don't you at least sit down and give it a try?"

"Maybe everyone *else* does, but *I don't!*" Ryker insists. "I'm *different.*"

Not wishing to deny his unique character, I relent. "Okay, after breakfast then." My son sits his naked bottom on a kitchen chair.

Five minutes into his cereal, Ryker calls to me in the laundry room, where I am wrestling the day's clothing out of the dryer. "Mama, I need you!" he beckons.

"Coming . . ." I answer, "just let me find one more sock." I dig out a sixth what-used-to-pass-as-white sock and rush to the kitchen.

"There's urine on my chair," Ryker bemoans. "Will you get me a rag, please?"

"I *knew* we should have tried to go to the potty before breakfast," I can't help but sigh in reply.

"But there was no urine in my penis before breakfast, Mom. It was in my bladder, but it wasn't ready to come out then, and then it just rushed right through my penis before I could catch it!" Ryker explains, in his usual rational tone. *A child this articulate really ought to be trained by now,* I think to myself. Just then I hear Traven, whom I have nicknamed "Bruiser" for his ornery temper and rough way of handling even his affection, coming down the stairs.

"I'm *not* going potty! I'm *not* going potty! I'm *not* going potty!" he intones loudly, bumping down the stairs on his hind quarters, one step at a time. "I'm going outside to play Batman and Robin," he announces as he pops into the kitchen, already headed for the sliding-glass door leading out to the patio. I sigh and let him pass. I know from experience that this is a battle not worth fighting. Traven has become so opposed to the idea of pottying that my tactic is to ignore the issue entirely, allowing him to assert his fiercely independent spirit in hopes that my acquiescence will temper his stubbornness. To force the issue with Traven would merely firm his resolve.

Cayden, my middle triplet, is a compliant, easygoing child. He likes to please me, and takes pleasure in his role as the sweetest and most generous of the brothers. He doesn't share their iron wills, and for a long time, seemed not to have a resistant bone in his yard-high body—until he began toilet training!

I hear Cayden coming down the stairs, quietly humming a Winnie-the-Pooh song. He is relaxed, content, peaceful. I meet him at the bottom of the stairs, holding out a new pair of Pull-Ups. "Come on, Punkin, let's go potty and put on some nice dry pants," I suggest gently. "You are getting so grown up!" I add, for a little extra motivational boost. "Nooooooo!" he whines, his pleasant smile turning suddenly sour. "I don't *want* to go on the potty. Nooooo!" he begins to cry. I take his hand and pull him into the bathroom, plying him with a promise of a story while he sits and tries. He sniffles a little, but complies, and sits for five minutes while I spin a tale about monsters in dark caves with pretty flowers all around, just like his favorite literary hero, Ferdinand the Bull. "I'm done," he reports suddenly, as soon as the story has ended. The potty bowl, as usual, is completely empty. He *never* goes. That is, until I put on a pair of dry Pull-Ups.

I have been through most of the Kubler-Ross emotional stages over this issue: denial, anger, bargaining, depression—yes, I have

Kerri Peterson

even shed tears over it. I rationalize that my children get so little of me, given the long hours I work, that they are desperate for care-taking and will snatch it up wherever they can get it. To have one's diaper changed is to feel like Mama is taking care of them. To sit down on the potty and do it themselves would not give the same pleasure. They *need* me. They need *more of me.* I consider cutting down to a four-day workweek in order to spend more time at home with them. I practice being truly present with them whenever I *am* home, which is not that often, given my every-third-night-on-call schedule and regular ten- to twelve-hour workdays. I try to resist the urge to get the laundry folded or the dishes done when I could be spending time with the boys.

No one goes to kindergarten in diapers, I've often been reassured by sympathetic friends and colleagues. I smile to myself as I collect wet Huggies from the bathroom floor and toss them into a plastic bag. "Do you know why Mama is so happy today?" I ask my three boys warmly. It is a ritual question, with which they are well familiar.

"Because you have *three beautiful boys!*" they answer in unison.

("Three beautiful *wet* boys," I am tempted to add.)

"Yes, I do," I affirm, gathering them into my arms for a group hug. "I certainly do."

On Becoming a Brother

Judy Margulis

I'VE WAITED NINETEEN YEARS TO WRITE THIS STORY. Our children don't live with us anymore. They're both college students, in different parts of the country, and although Hannah spent the summer after her freshman year at home with us, I wonder if we'll ever all live together again. Yesterday our family was at the beach. As we were leaving, I watched my children walking arm in arm, deep in conversation, and I marveled at their closeness. It wasn't always that way.

When my son Jacob was eighteen months old, I discovered I was pregnant with Hannah. My husband, Jeffrey, and I had decided to stop using birth control months before we really wanted to get pregnant, because it had taken a year to conceive the first time. I got pregnant that first month. Unlike our fantasy of having our children three years apart, we were about to have a two-year-old and a newborn.

We were in shock, but happy, and relieved not to revisit our previous worries of infertility. Jacob was an unusually articulate little boy, already talking in full and complex sentences, and was good at expressing his feelings. He could say when he was angry or frustrated, shy or scared. We would walk into a room with a lot of people and Jacob, hiding his head in my shoulder, would say, "I feel shy, Mommy." We knew his language skills would be a great help when his sister was born. We talked with him a lot about the baby who was due to arrive and what it would be like to be a big brother. Jacob was very excited.

Our daughter, Hannah, was born when Jacob was twenty-seven months old. At first he was very excited and very loving toward her. But within a few weeks it became clear to him that Hannah was not capable of being his playmate, that she was here to stay, and that she was taking his mommy's attention away from him. Jacob became quite tense. One day, sitting in his car seat, he said, "I . . . I . . . I . . . want . . . to . . . to . . . to . . . ge . . . ge . . . get . . . out . . . of . . . of . . . of . . . the car."

Instead of expressing his disturbance with his usual passionate flair for words, he had begun to stutter. Now, he could not say "I'm angry at you, Daddy." Instead, he would falter, "I . . . I . . . I'm . . . ang . . . ang . . . ." We had worried about all sorts of responses to the birth of his new sibling, but never this. It seemed like the worst reaction possible. It was so painful to witness our beautifully articulate boy struggling to get even the simplest sentence out, fumbling for the words.

Several days after the onset of Jacob's stuttering, Jeffrey and I decided that Jacob needed some quality time with his mother. Jeffrey took Hannah and a bottle of goat's milk for a long outing and left Jacob and me alone in the house. I was watching him play with his trucks in his room when I said to him, "It's really hard to be a big brother isn't it?" Jacob stopped what he was doing, looked at me, burst into tears, and said, without stumbling over one word, "I hate it! And I want Hannah to go back in your tummy!" He cried hard while I held him and reassured him of the love that his daddy and I felt for him. I was so relieved that he could finally express the forbidden feelings, the feelings that didn't feel compatible to him with being a good big brother. My son never stuttered again.

The Box

Rebecca Boucher

I SENT A BOX OF MY DAUGHTER'S CLOTHES to a friend of mine in New Orleans. Her husband referred to the box as "a major form of diplomatic exchange and currency among women belonging to separate sovereignties." No, I said, not exactly. More like a ceremony for the end of toddlerhood in a society that has no formal rite to mark that moment. His wife, Morrey, understood. She called when her kids were quiet and spoke gently to me. I know, she said, what this means, and I thank you.

I had been waiting to have a friend like her to receive that box. We all met this last summer in the Adirondacks. She, her husband, and their two small children were visiting her parents, who live a short walk from our summer house. I thought it would be smart of me to introduce myself, as I also had a three-year-old and we could share a baby-sitter. Our community there is so small that those of us relegated to the edge of the lake, the shallow section littered with swimmies and empty juice boxes, ought to form alliances. That way, when we look toward the end of the dock, by the deep water, where the older children's mothers sit with summer novels and thermoses of Bloody Marys for the four-o'clock cocktail call, there is less chance of a disgruntled, mutinous uprising that could turn ugly.

The Box

I didn't expect to like Morrey as much as I did. I knew she was an ex-ballerina, which I maturely decided not to hold against her, me with my thoughts that perhaps this was the summer to give in and order one of the skirted bathing suits from the Vermont Country Store catalog. It turned out Morrey was quick—not only on her feet, but with words. She was always up for an outing and brought extra snacks. In the first weeks of the summer, while we were making friends at a breakneck speed, we sort of ignored the children. We watched them to make sure they weren't drowning, but didn't spend a lot of time supervising their parallel play and introducing them to shore birds. I believe, in retrospect, that this was the secret to their success. While we were making friends, so were my daughter, Faith, and her son, Henry. And I am not speaking here of mere playmates: they discovered each other, deeply and seriously. They became friends of the heart.

I noticed, around mid-July, that the first thing Faith would do upon waking was ask for Henry. She is a stubborn little thing, and wouldn't give up asking until she got a clear, concrete answer as to when the next meeting would take place. More than once, she started on her own out the driveway when told he wasn't available immediately. "I'll just go check," she'd toss over her shoulder as she set out toward his house.

I started keeping a closer eye on them. It was clear they shared a bond entirely of their own making. When Henry made his appearance, they would join hands and go to the screened-in porch, where they sat on the floor facing each other. There, they would engage in imaginary play, often using little figures and plastic animals to people their world. There were times of silence, when each seemed to understand what the other was doing intuitively, and times of great chattering and laughing. They built special hiding places, usually involving the dark places under tables or beneath the cedar tree that grows outside my kitchen window. Once, while they shared a sandwich on the beach, Henry reached over and softly brushed crumbs off Faith's face. His touch was so tender, so gentle, that there could be no mistake that these two had found a place of comfort with each other that few friends do. They enjoyed running through the sprinklers, sometimes laughing so hard they fell down on the grass.

It was a hot summer and clothes were often left discarded on the lawn, impediments to comfort. I have a wonderful snapshot of the two of them: Faith naked and Henry in soaked shorts, having a deep discussion, their wet hair plastered to their heads. Faith gesticulates wildly and Henry looks deep into her eyes, transfixed.

What were they were discussing at that particular moment? At three, there would not seem to be that much on the menu. World affairs, real estate prices, educational philosophy weren't of interest. As far was they were concerned, the tennis round-robin and Saturday sailing races didn't even exist. They weren't worried about what to make for supper or whether or not this was the summer they would finally be invited to the Kennedys' party. From my standpoint, that left little to discuss. Whenever I got close enough to overhear them, it was as if they were speaking in tongues. I couldn't understand a word. Watching them, Morrey and I laughed and wondered what they had to say to each other. Henry's grandmother cocked an eyebrow at us. "You two aren't the only ones who can be friends," she said. "Three-year-olds can have soul mates, too."

This fall, as I was going through Faith's overstuffed drawers, I found a way to keep something of that summer—something of both the friendship and the fleeting days of toddlerhood—alive. Who better than Henry's little sister to wear Faith's special smocked dress and that little size-two sweater set with the roses, for which I paid dearly and which I loved every time Faith wore it? Of course, it was not about the clothes as much as the memories. And it was not about the memories as much as it was about turning your back on what has become the past, realizing there will never be a two-year-old in your house again, that there will never be anyone to fit into those little pink t-strap shoes. I had to cull those clothes and they had to go somewhere. I could have donated them to charity. But I wanted to know that those little pieces of her toddlerhood were somewhere I could visit or see. I needed to let go and yet couldn't.

One might think I've had enough of toddlers: I have had four children over twelve years. I spaced them so that the youngest could open the door to an airplane bathroom alone before I gave birth to the next. While this made traveling easier, it has also meant constantly contending with a toddler in the house. I have changed diapers for most of those twelve years and am alarmed to see how Gina on *Sesame Street* has aged. My first high-school-aged baby-sitter has her own children now. To a certain degree, I have had enough. Toddlers are messy and I am, by nature, a neat person. I have lived most of my adult years with Cheerios on the floor and sippy cups in my pocketbook. I am physically uncomfortable if I don't have wipes in my purse at all times. Buckling car seats is something I can do with one hand.

Even so, with your last child, each milestone is a jewel added reluctantly to your necklace of memories. The first steps, the first words, the day she climbed to the top of the jungle gym are obvious gems. How about the sight of her on the beach as Henry reached over to brush those crumbs away? Or when she dressed up as Little Red Riding Hood and the dog played the Big Bad Wolf, wearing an old nightie? I remember the weight of her head on my shoulder when she fell asleep in my arms. The summer she wanted to hear *The Story About Ping* over and over and over until we all played hot potato with the book and could recite it by memory. I can see her running unsteadily across the grass in that little dress, the one with the rick-rack along the hem that I bought at a yard sale. I am proud of her growth and measure it, physically at least, on the back of the basement door, as I did with the rest of her siblings. *See, Faith, Jamie was this tall when he was your age. Some day you'll be as tall as Annie.* In reality, I'm looking at the marks closer to the floor. *Look, Faith, remember when you were only this big? I do.*

There is no ceremony to mark this moment, mostly because it's not a point in time but a sneaking, gradual change that happens when you're not looking. It occurs while you're busy planning the next vacation or working on the PTA fund-raiser or going through the box of snow boots in the basement hoping to find a pair that will fit this year. You pack enough lunch boxes and sign enough permission slips and comfort a child through another bout of the flu and you're there. Your baby is a toddler and then, poof, a toddler no more.

Henry's little sister loved the pink t-strap shoes. Morrey told me about how she put them on and danced down the hall, pointing at them. Another memory for another mother's necklace. I kept the little dress with the rick-rack on the hem.

Acknowledgments

I sometimes think that my daughter, Athena, like the baby dragon in *My Father's Dragon,* fell into her toddlerhood from a cloud in the sky. At two she graces the Wild Island of our home speaking in full sentences, going to the bathroom by herself, and pretending "you're the baby and I'm the mommy, okay?" Without any prompting, Athena has always been exquisitely polite and kind. "Tsank you Mommy," she says as I hand her a cup of juice or kiss away a hurt. Lying still for her pajamas Athena looks at me very seriously: "I cooperate," she whispers. "Thank you," I whisper back. "Tsank you too," she answers.

I have many, many people to thank for helping this book come into being. First and foremost, thank you to the contributors whose stories fill these pages and to the hundreds of other parents, grandparents, and caretakers who shared their toddler tales with me. Thank you to those very toddlers whose messy, chaotic, and energetic presence inspires us to rage at them, adore them, and write about them, and to my own two toddlers: Hesperus and Athena. Thank you to my parents: Lynn Margulis and Thomas N. Margulis; my brothers: Dorion Sagan, Jeremy Sagan, and Zachary Margulis-Ohnuma; and my little sister, Katherine Starkman Margulis, who have given me lots of life material. My warm thanks to Abi Morales who cared for me as a toddler and who tells me

Acknowledgments

I spoke my first words with a Spanish accent, and also to Susan Gries, Brianne Goodspeed, Jim Propis, Susan Buscaglia and Hannah Margulis-Kessel who all did more than I have space to mention here and who could often be found at our house playing with my munchkins while I disappeared upstairs to work. My thanks also to Alix Kennedy, Nicole Cooley, Loune Viaud, Paul Kivel, Michelle Korman, Janet Tolg, Sally Ahearn, François Gobillard, Andrew Singer, Ashisha, Karen and Mark Driscoll, Ericka Lutz, Joyce Maynard, Octavia Butler, Judith Hooper, Max Page, Eve Weinbaum, and my editor at Seal, Ingrid Emerick, for their support, enthusiasm, and good ideas.

Without the hard work and acumen extraordinaire of my agent, Stephanie von Hirschberg, this book would not have come into being; and without the encouragement of both my dearest Nola and my Auntie Judy it would not even have completed its gestation. Thank you both. Thank you also to Frances Smith Foster (who finished a term paper sitting on a pile of newspapers while in labor with her firstborn and seems to have set an example for her students) and the many other wonderful professors and students at Emory University. Thank you to Henry Louis Gates, Jr., my college mentor, for sending me down this writerly path in the first place.

My husband, James di Properzio, has contributed more than just a story to this anthology. I am indebted to him for his patience, enthusiasm, and support, and for his careful reading and keen-eyed editing. It was he who whisked my daughters off to the park, the library, or the museum so I could have the space to write and edit, who brought me red tea and chocolate late at night, and who got me into this toddler mess in the first place. Tsank you.

About the Contributors

Mary Jane Beaufrand lives in Seattle with her husband, Juan, and two *vagabundos:* Sofia (age three) and Ricky (age one). A graduate of the Bennington Creative Writing Seminars, she has published fiction and creative nonfiction in *Web del Sol, Short Story Magazine Online,* and *Fables Magazine,* among others. Ricky sleeps well now and enjoys dropping things. Mary Jane and Sofia are back in music class. Most evenings you can catch all four of them dancing around the living room to "Love Shack."

Yvette Bonaparte grew up in New Jersey, but left after college in search of better weather. A former modern dancer, she used her master's degree in Writing to teach at Skyline College and the University of San Francisco. Currently, she is an administrator at the San Francisco Friends School. Addicted to travel since she lived in Liberia as a child, she has trekked through Nepal, ridden camels in Egypt, and been pregnant on Kauai and Oahu, where her son, Liam, was born. Her short fiction has appeared in *Writing for Our Lives* and *Kalliope.* She lives in San Francisco with her husband and son, and does her best writing when everyone in the house is asleep.

Rebecca Boucher lives in Brooklyn with her husband and four children.

David Carkeet is a linguist by training, a novelist, and the father of Anne, Laurie, and Molly. His novels include *The Full Catastrophe* and *The Error of Our Ways*. He has published essays in the *New York Times Book Review*, the *Oxford American*, the *Village Voice*, and elsewhere.

Samuel P. Clark is Chief of Operations for a social-service agency and has served as a city commissioner for fourteen years. His work has been anthologized in *Blow-Drying the Frog & Other Parenting Adventures*, the *Don't Sweat Stories*, and *A 5th Portion of Chicken Soup for the Soul*. His annual tradition of writing a Father's Day message was featured in *Woman's World*. He lives in north-central Florida with wife, April Burk, and daughters Kayla (now ten) and Sophie (four).

Nicole Cooley grew up in New Orleans and lives in New Jersey with her husband and toddler. Her first book of poetry, *Resurrection*, won the 1995 Walt Whitman Award from the Academy of American Poets. Her novel, *Judy Garland, Ginger Love*, was published by HarperCollins in 1998 and her second book of poetry, *The Afflicted Girls*, about the Salem witch trials of 1692, is forthcoming from Louisiana State University Press. An assistant professor of English at Queens College, CUNY, she has held fellowships from the American Antiquarian Society and the National Endowment for the Arts.

About the Contributors

Dennis Donoghue's work has appeared in *Teacher Magazine,* the *Brandeis Review, The Sun,* and other magazines and literary journals. A sixth-grade teacher at Salisbury Elementary School, he writes early in the morning, before the sun and his toddlers are up. He lives in Rowley, Massachusetts, with his wife, Carla, and their three daughters.

Karen Crafts Driscoll gave birth to four children in less than four years (one of whom weighed almost twelve pounds). Her writing about mothering has been published in the best-selling *Chicken Soup* series, *Chocolate for a Woman's Courage, Chocolate for a Woman's Blessings* and *Chocolate for a Woman's Soul, Vol. 2.* She has also been published in *Mothering Magazine; Brain, Child; ePregnancy;* and elsewhere. Karen and her family live in Wallingford, Connecticut, where she has been known to make an amaretto cheesecake so scrumptious that those who taste it remember it for years to come.

Hope Edelman is the author of three nonfiction books, including the best-seller *Motherless Daughters: The Legacy of Loss,* which was a *New York Times* Notable Book of the Year. She is the recipient of a Pushcart Prize for creative nonfiction. Her essays and articles have appeared in the *New York Times,* the *Chicago Tribune,* the *San Francisco Chronicle, Self, Glamour, Child,* and *Seventeen.* She is currently writing her fourth book, *Motherless Mothers,* about parenting. She lives with her husband and two daughters in southern California.

Louise Erdrich is the author of *The Master Butchers Singing Club,*

Love Medicine, The Beet Queen, Tracks, The Bingo Palace, Blue Jay's Dance, and two volumes of poetry. She is the coauthor, with her late husband, Michael Dorris, of *The Crown of Columbus.* She lives in Minnesota with her six children.

Peter W. Fong lives in Pray, Montana, with his wife, Sarah Putnam, and their two children: Dave (age nine) and Marina (age five). His fiction has been published in the *Onion River Review, Soundings East,* and *Tumblewords.* Accounts of his family's recent travels in Asia have appeared in *Fly Fisherman* and the *New York Times.* He won the 25th Anniversary Fiction Prize from *Soundings East,* and has held a Moran Fellowship at Yellowstone National Park, as well as a Montana Arts Council creative writing fellowship. The grandson of a Chinese laundryman, Fong has worked as a copyeditor, high-school teacher, commercial fisherman, and sportfishing guide.

Putnam Goodwin-Boyd was an elementary-school teacher for ten years before taking a hiatus to care for his three young children, get a master's degree from Smith College, and write. He has published a math text for English as a Second Language students and written for *Connecticut College Magazine, Hampshire Life*, and *FamilyFun.* He has also written children's fiction for *Cricket* and *Spider Magazine.*

Katie Greenebaum graduated from Yale and received an M.F.A. from the University of Virginia, where she was a Henry Hoyns Fellow in fiction writing and won the Balch Award for best short story. She has been a Pushcart Prize finalist and has published in journals such as *Chelsea* and *Literal Latte,* and the anthology *Child of Mine.* An English and writing teacher, she lives with her husband, Josh May, and their children, Nora, Jake, and Alice, in Nashville, Tennessee.

Geoff Griffin is a sportswriter who lives in Enterprise, Utah, with his wife and two children. He enjoys being home with his daughter, Alex (age twelve), and son, Mose (age ten), during the day before going off to cover ballgames late into the night.

Elisabeth Rose Gruner is Associate Professor of English and Women's Studies at the University of Richmond, where she teaches children's literature. In addition to publishing scholarly articles on children's literature and Victorian novels, she writes frequently for *Brain, Child.* Nick is now five, and his big sister, Mariah, is thirteen.

Ayun Halliday is the author of *The Big Rumpus* and the brains, breastmilk, and sole employee of the *East Village Inky,* which won the 2002 Firecracker Alternative Book Award for best 'zine. She contributes regularly to *BUST* and *Hip Mama,* but rarely to the upkeep of her small apartment in Brooklyn. A collection of Ayun's autobiographical travel memoirs, *No Touch Monkey! And Other Travel Lessons Learned Too Late,* about her travels in Sumatra, Rwanda, Saigon, and elsewhere, is forthcoming from Seal Press.

Shu-Huei Henrickson absconded from her homeland Taiwan and entered the U.S. (legally) in 1991. She lives in Illinois and teaches English at Rock Valley College. Prone to frequent attacks of wanderlust, she has traveled to Russia, Japan, Malaysia, Turkey, England, Germany, Norway, and elsewhere. Her writing has appeared in *Standards, American Voices, Fourth Genre, Towers, Mind in Motion, Spectacle, Out of Line,* and *Fiction International.*

Kerry Herlihy's stories have been published in *The Bitch in the House* and *Motherland: Writings by Irish-Americans on Mothers and Daughters.* She currently teaches English as a Second Language in southern Maine, where she and her daughter live.

Leanna James is a widely published writer based in Northampton, Massachusetts. A frequent contributor to *Brain, Child,* she has an M.F.A. in creative writing from Mills College. A former college creative writing and literature teacher, she is currently at work on a novel set in San Francisco about a musician struggling to reconcile with her estranged mother.

Alexandra Kennedy is Vice President and Editorial Director of *FamilyFun* and *Disney Magazine.* Since *FamilyFun's* premier in 1991, she has overseen its editorial content as well as its brand extensions, including a best-selling book series and an award-winning Web site, and has appeared regularly on television. With a B.A. from Colgate University and an M.F.A. in poetry from the University of Massachusetts, she began her magazine career as an editor at *New England Monthly,* two-time winner of the National

Magazine Award. She lives in Northampton, Massachusetts, with her husband, poet James Haug, and their two sons.

Paul Kivel is a social justice activist, writer, and violence-prevention educator. His most recent books include *Boys Will Be Men: Raising Our Sons for Courage, Caring, and Community; I Can Make My World a Safer Place: A Kid's Book about Stopping Violence;* and *Uprooting Racism: How White People Can Work for Racial Justice,* which won the 1996 Gustavus Myers Award for best book on human rights. He lives in northern California.

Gordon Korman is an author of books for children and young adults. Born in Montreal, Quebec, he published his first novel, *This Can't Be Happening at MacDonald Hall,* when he was fourteen. He has written over forty books and won many awards, including the Manitoba Young Readers' Choice Award for *The Zucchini Warriors,* the Markham Civic Award for the Arts, and the ALA Best Book List and ALA Editor's Choice for *A Semester in the Life of a Garbage Bag.* Translated into French, Swedish, Norwegian, and Cantonese, his books have sold over seven million copies. He lives with his wife, Michelle, and their children, Jay (age four) and Daisy (age one), on Long Island.

Ericka Lutz is the author of seven books, including *On the Go with Baby* and *The Complete Idiot's Guide to Stepparenting.* She has written about parenting for anthologies (*Child of Mine*), periodicals (*Parents Press, Chicago Baby*), and the Web (Amazon.com, Baby-

Zone.com). An instructor at UC Berkeley and a writing consultant, she lives with her husband and their nine-year-old daughter in Oakland, California. She contends she's still cool, though her daughter, Annie, is beginning to express doubts.

Judy Margulis is a psychologist in private practice in Berkeley, California. She lives in Oakland with her husband, Jeffrey Kessel. She has a son, Jacob, twenty-three, and a daughter, Hannah, twenty-one.

Joyce Maynard has been a journalist and fiction writer since her teens. She is the author of four novels, a memoir, a collection of personal essays on mothering, and two picture books, as well as hundreds of columns and essays for the *New York Times,* National Public Radio, and many magazines. Maynard wrote *Parenting Magazine's* column "A Mother's Days" for many years, as well as the syndicated column "Domestic Affairs," in which the story here first appeared. The son whose first steps she describes recently turned nineteen. Her latest novel, *The Usual Rules,* includes a four-year-old boy coping with the sudden death of his mother. "Among my goals as a writer," she says, "is to portray children with at least as much dignity and understanding for the complexity of childhood as an adult can muster."

Morrey McElroy is a theater teacher, children's theater playwright, and mother of two in New Orleans, Louisiana. She has an M.F.A. from Louisiana State University.

About the Contributors

Priscilla Leigh McKinley graduated from the University of Iowa with an M.F.A. in Nonfiction Writing and is currently working on a Ph.D. in Language, Literacy, and Culture. Her creative nonfiction has been published in a variety of magazines and books, including *Between Mothers and Sons: Women Writers Speak about Having Sons and Raising Men*. She is working on a memoir, Bittersweet Vines, about losing her sight and regaining her independence. She lives in Iowa City with her husband, son (who is now a teenager), dog, and two ferrets.

Marie Myung-Ok Lee has written six novels for children, including *Necessary Roughness*, an American Library Association Best Book for Young Adults. Her work has also appeared in the *Kenyon Review*, *American Voice*, and the *New York Times*, and her short fiction won an O. Henry citation. She has been a Fulbright scholar, a founder of the Asian American Writers' Workshop, and is currently a visiting scholar at Brown University.

Catherine Newman is a freelance writer and editor who lives with her family in western Massachusetts. A contributing editor at *FamilyFun*, she published an essay about marriage in the best-selling collection *The Bitch in the House*, and has written extensively about toddlers in her weekly on-line parenting journal, "Bringing Up Ben," on parentcenter.com, where part of her essay was originally published.

Jennifer Niesslein is coeditor of the award-winning magazine *Brain, Child*. She lives with her family in Charlottesville, Virginia.

Brett Paesel is an actress and writer. She has written a pilot for Comedy Central and numerous sketches for the live sketch show *Margot's Bush*. Formerly in the cast of HBO's *Mr. Show with Bob and David*, she currently does performance pieces around town. She lives in Los Angeles with her husband, Patrick Towne, and their son, two-year-old Spencer.

Elise Paschen is the author of *Houses: Coasts* and *Infidelities*, winner of the Nicholas Roerich Poetry Prize. Her poems have been widely anthologized and published in numerous magazines and journals, including the *New Yorker*, the *New Republic*, and the *Nation*. A cofounder of the Poetry in Motion program that places poetry posters in subways and buses, Paschen is coeditor of *Poetry in Motion* and *Poetry in Motion from Coast to Coast*, as well as the best-selling anthology *Poetry Speaks*. Former Executive Director of the Poetry Society of America, she teaches at the School of the Art Institute of Chicago. She lives in Chicago with her husband and their two children.

Jamie Pearson wrote "The Dinner Hour" to regain her sanity after an evening that tested her both as a parent and a person. She came to writing via a degree in political science and a career selling securities on Wall Street. She now works as a freelance journalist, writing for the *Rockridge News* and the *Oakland Business Review*. In her current position as a full-time mother of two, she struggles daily to understand how the most fulfilling work of her life can also be the most mind-numbing. She lives with her family in Menlo Park, California.

About the Contributors

Kerri Peterson is a family physician in Carmel Valley, California. She is the mother of four boys under seven, and is currently on sabbatical from medicine, in order to be at home with her children. She has a regular advice column in *Working Mother* magazine and has been a regular columnist for *Single Mom* magazine, as well as for *Medical Economics*. She has also written essays for several medical journals about the humanistic side of medical practice. She is writing a memoir about her experiences as a physician in recovery from anorexia and drug addiction.

James di Properzio attended St. John's College in Santa Fe and Annapolis. Currently he frails the banjo, plucks the lute, blows the shakuhachi, draws, and writes prose, poetry, and creative nonfiction from his home in Greenfield, Massachusetts. When he is not taking care of his two toddlers, he is advocating green local politics and putting them into practice as a member of the Board of Directors of Green Fields Market, the local food co-op. As the founder of a writing consulting business, Properzio Prose, he also writes science profiles for the *World & I* magazine, edits scientific texts, and translates Italian.

Scott Samuelson drinks not-too-dry gin martinis, spends too much on the food he cooks, is especially fond of the music of Ben Webster, and, when not too tired at the end of the day, types an essay or poem on an old Smith Corona. He and his wife, Helen, are raising their daughter, Irene, and son, Billy, in southeastern Iowa. When not at home chasing after his children or traveling in his grandfather's native Lebanon, he is teaching courses at Kirkwood Community College in

Philosophy, Logic, or the Humanities. He has published scholarly articles on James Joyce, Vico, and Italian mannerist philosophers.

Erika Schickel is a writer, performer, and teacher. Her work has appeared in the *LA Weekly, Hip Mama, BUST,* and in the anthology *Another City: Writing from Los Angeles.* Her play, *Wild Amerika,* has been broadcast on public radio stations internationally. She lives in Los Angeles with her husband and two daughters.

Suzanne Schryver is a full-time mother of three small children: Cameron (four and a half), Justine (almost three), and Wesley (fifteen months). She lives in New Hampshire where she volunteers at her children's preschool and is an avid runner, even in the worst weather. Before becoming a mother, she taught creative writing and earned a black belt in karate.

Meredith Small is a writer and professor of anthropology at Cornell University. She is the author of *Our Babies, Ourselves: How Biology and Culture Shape the Way We Parent* and *KIDS: How Biology and Culture Shape the Way We Raise Our Children.*

Annie Spiegelman is First Assistant Director in the Directors Guild of America and the author of *Annie's Garden Journal: Reflections on Roses, Weeds, Men and Life*—listed as a Border's Original Voices selection—and *Growing Seasons: Half-baked Garden Tips, Cheap Advice on Marriage and Questionable Theories on Motherhood.* She lives in northern California with her family.

About the Contributors

Marian Brown Sprague is on an extended leave of absence from her work in the nonprofit sector. For the past five years, her job satisfaction has come from mothering her only daughter. Her writing has been published in the *San Jose Mercury News,* the *Santa Clara Weekly, Who Cares,* and *Caring People.* She lives with her family in Woodside, California.

Sachin Waikar fled clinical psychology—where his anxiety research was published in several journals and featured on national television—and business consulting for the risk-free life of a writer. His current projects include a short-story collection about suburban Indian Americans and screenplays about high-functioning zombies and spy-dreaming dads. Sachin lives in the western suburbs of Chicago with his wife, Kalpana, and son, Kayan.

Eve S. Weinbaum used to have lots of time for union and community organizing. She is now the mother of Jonah, who is four, and Aviva, three. In her free time she is an assistant professor of Labor Studies at the University of Massachusetts at Amherst. Her book, *To Move a Mountain,* is forthcoming from the New Press. She has published several articles on grassroots organizing, women and politics, and social movements. She lives in Amherst, Massachusetts.

About the Editor

Jennifer Margulis Ph.D. is a widely published freelance writer, writing consultant, and photojournalist. She has a B.A. from Cornell University, an M.A. from UC Berkeley, and a Ph.D. from Emory University. She has taught courses in nineteenth-century American and African-American literature at Brenau University, Emory University, Mount Holyoke College, and elsewhere; published a wide range of scholarly articles; and coedited a classroom edition of Susanna Haswell Rowson's 1794 play, *Slaves in Algiers.* She has also eaten fried crickets in Niger, appeared live on primetime TV in France, and performed the cancan in America. She lives with her family in western Massachusetts.

Selected Titles from Seal Press

Mother Shock: Loving Every (Other) Minute of It by Andrea J. Buchanan. $14.95, 1-58005-082-4. One new mom's refreshing and down-to-earth look at the birth of a mother.

The Big Rumpus: A Mother's Tales from the Trenches by Ayun Halliday. $15.95, 1-58005-071-9. Creator of the wildly popular *East Village Inky*, Halliday describes the quirks and everyday travails of a young urban family, warts and all.

Growing Seasons: Half-baked Garden Tips, Cheap Advice on Marriage and Questionable Theories on Motherhood by Annie Spiegelman. $14.95, 1-58005-079-4. A celebration of family in all its comfort and complexity.

The Mother Trip: Hip Mama's Guide to Staying Sane in the Chaos of Motherhood by Ariel Gore. $14.95, 1-58005-029-8. In a book that is part self-help, part critique of the mommy myth, and part hip-mama handbook, Ariel Gore offers support to mothers who break the mold.

Breeder: Real-Life Stories from the New Generation of Mothers edited by Ariel Gore and Bee Lavender, foreword by Dan Savage. $16.00, 1-58005-051-4. From the editors of Hip Mama, this hilarious and heartrending compilation creates a space where Gen-X moms can dish, cry, scream, and laugh.

Seal Press publishes many books of fiction and nonfiction by women writers. Please visit our Web site at www.sealpress.com.